Nontoxic Masculinity

Nontoxic Masculinity

Jessica Chasteen

Copyright

Published by Garden Variety Press

Print Book (Paperback) ISBN: 979-8-9995250-2-4

First Edition

Disclaimer: This book is designed to provide information and motivation to readers. It is sold with the understanding that the publisher is not engaged to render any type of psychological, legal, or any other kind of professional advice. The content is the sole expression and opinion of the author. No warranties or guarantees are expressed or implied by the publisher's choice to include any of the content in this volume.

For more information about the author and her work, visit: nontoxicmen.org and gardenvarietyblog.com

Content Warning

This book addresses sensitive topics related to men's mental health and personal development, including discussions of suicide, substance abuse, sexual assault, domestic violence, and other forms of trauma. While these topics are approached with care and in the context of healing and growth, readers who may be triggered by such content are encouraged to prioritize their well-being.

If you or someone you know is struggling with thoughts of self-harm, please reach out for help:

- National Suicide Prevention Lifeline: 988
- Crisis Text Line: Text HOME to 741741
- National Domestic Violence Hotline: 1-800-799-7233

This book is intended to celebrate healthy masculinity and provide positive pathways forward. It is not a substitute for professional mental health care, therapy, or medical treatment.

Dedication

This book is dedicated to three very special men in particular:

- My dad, Reverend Eddie Chasteen, who taught me the love of the Father,
- My friend, Bassem Youssef, who taught me courage and authenticity in storytelling, and
- My husband, Jaime Alvarez, who taught me appreciation of the whole man with his shadow.

Prologue

According to the American Institute for Boys and Men (AIBM), men in this country are experiencing a tragic mental health and identity crisis, with very high opiate overdose rates and 4x the number of suicides than women. Not only that, but men and boys are also struggling in school and the workplace, leading them to feel "useless" or lonely or both. This has happened because the broader cultural shift towards women's equality has unintentionally led to a neglecting of the male psyche.

Boys and men have been vilified for being "toxic" when they've never been given a blueprint of how to be or act in this new cultural reality. We've been treating gender dynamics like a zero sum game, in which if women have MORE power, then men must have LESS. But that model is only applicable in the small minority of spaces with fixed numbers of seats at the table (like the US Senate). The majority of spaces can and should include both male and female perspectives, talents, and voices. After all, men matter, too.

But what do these words toxic and nontoxic even mean? Think about a box of crayons. If the crayons are nontoxic, then that means they won't cause harm. They're **safe**. That's what it means to be a nontoxic person, too! It means I can feel safe around you. I can trust that you won't harm me.

Toxic masculinity — the type of masculinity that harms women, children, and other men — is a very real and present danger, and this book does not in any way attempt to downplay this reality. Instead, I hope to provide a hopeful alternative vision for detoxifying the future by learning from good men — not perfect, but still good — in the present, the past, and our myths, who overcame their common struggles with toxicity through virtue and demonstrated shared strengths and gifts that will inspire men toward healing on a collective level. The only way to end toxic masculinity is to treat it like a disease that is poisoning the hearts and minds of our men, and offer a path to detox.

This is also not a book that seeks to tell men how to be more like women. Many men long to be considered safe, so much so that they will portray themselves as feminine or put on the "gay voice" to put women at ease. These are valiant efforts, but as Richard Reeves, founder of the AIBM, has pointed out on more than one occasion: too often men feel that to become "nontoxic" means to become more feminine. This cultural and psychological misunderstanding is doing a huge disservice to both men and women.

I'm writing this book as a celebration of good men. But it's also a book for men who want to become the best versions of themselves and for any person who wants to understand masculinity better. But how can I, a woman, explain to you how to become a better man? Because I am a storyteller, and I love to tell of the myths and legends and histories of brilliant men so that we can all learn from them. Sometimes to understand who we are, we must explore who we have always been.

It's important to realize that "masculinity" is an energy, a way of being and acting out the stories of our lives. It is most often associated with men and manliness, but people of all genders can and do experience masculine energy and exhibit masculine behaviors. The same is true for femininity. Sometimes we call this our "feminine and masculine sides." We have both these aspects to our personality because every single one of us has both a mother and a father — or we wouldn't exist! We all have been influenced by both men and women throughout our lives and even through our DNA.

This book is based around the twelve enduring "archetypes" of men. Archetypes are characters from stories that have the same patterns in the kinds of conflicts they'll face and lessons they'll learn. The archetypes we'll discuss in this book include the following:

- The Warrior
- The Magician
- The King
- The Lover
- The Joker
- The Hero
- The Caregiver
- The Sage
- The Explorer
- The Innocent
- The Rebel
- The Creator

Each of these archetypes embodies a powerful truth about what it means to be human, but especially what it means to be a man. There will be many women who recognize their own masculine sides in these pages, so consider a yin yang symbol and how the light side contains a portion of dark, and the dark side contains a portion of light. This is how gender energy works, too. Every man has femininity in him. Every woman has masculinity in her. This is because we all contain our father and our mother.

I'm sure there will be a few who think I'm wrong to attribute certain struggles or strengths to men specifically and not be inclusive of women as well. But the truth is: men and women are both different and the same, like a Venn diagram. For example, if I ask you to imagine someone with commitment issues, who do you imagine, a man or woman? Most likely a man, but that doesn't mean zero women have commitment issues - it just means it is a characteristic that trends male. If I ask you to imagine an adrenaline junkie, which sex are they?

Is it surprising to know that fewer than 1 in 5 professional skydivers are women? What about if I ask you to imagine a rebel, a warrior, a king? Again, there are strengths and struggles that men tend to share more than women do (and vice versa), and it's important to acknowledge, discuss, and respect these differences.

I'm not writing this book to exclude women. In fact, y'all deserve your own book of your own archetypes who demonstrate feminine conflicts and healing, like the Huntress, the Crone, and the Queen. In the divine feminine list, there is overlap in the Lover, the Sage, and the Caregiver, so many women may see themselves in those chapters of this book, but I have taken great care to focus on men for this project because I have seen the negative effects of men being told what toxic masculinity is but not what nontoxic masculinity is. I hope there is a lesson for everyone in each chapter because even if it doesn't apply to you, dear reader, it might help you understand someone in your life a little bit better.

For each archetype in this book, we will explore examples of some of my favorite men across time, from Sun Tzu to Steve Irwin to Jesus of Nazareth to Fred Rogers, and discuss events in world history that were brought about by divine masculine energy. There will be some tough love in here for toxic folks, so put on your big boy pants and buckle up. I promise not to hit too hard (for a girl). At the end of each chapter, there will be time to stop and reflect on your own masculinity and self development.

Don't just be a real man.

Be a real **good** man.

Contents

The Warrior

Overview

- **Description:** The Warrior embodies discipline, protection, and action. This archetype is about mastery, focus, and the ability to overcome obstacles.
- **Major Conflict:** The Warrior struggles with balancing destruction and preservation. He risks becoming either overly aggressive (Abuser) or self-defeating (Defector).
- **Path to Growth:** The Warrior becomes his best self by being accountable to his community, practicing self-discipline, and using his strength to protect others.

Stories of the Warrior

"A true warrior fights not because he hates what is in front of him, but because he loves what is behind him." -G.K. Chesterton

Masculinity is the greatest destructive force on the planet. Yeah, I said it. But hold on! I may not mean what you think I mean. By contrast, femininity is a creative, life-giving force, but again, don't jump to conclusions that one of these energies is inherently positive while the other is inherently negative. That is simply not the case. There are both toxic and nontoxic examples of masculinity and femininity.

But how can creative be more toxic than destructive? It all depends on the context. What if I'm creating drama? What if I'm creating problems where they don't exist? What if I'm enlivening doubt or mistrust among the group? That's toxic femininity right there. But that's not what this book is about. This book is about **nontoxic** masculinity, so back to those benevolent destroyers.

When we consider the balance of all things, we can understand destruction as a necessary force. One could even call it kind, when properly administered. Imagine a garden abandoned by its gardener. Without mowing or hoeing, it's been choked out by weeds. Sure, the strongest specimens survived, but without pruning or mulching, even they are cruelly competing for nutrients and water. So what do mowing and hoeing and pruning and mulching have in common? They are controlled demolition. They are nontoxic, intentional destructive forces at play in our very own backyard.

Intentional destruction is the partner of intentional creation. They work beautifully in balance with each other. When I think about intentional destruction, I think about Michaelangelo, carving a sculpture out of a solid block of raw granite. I think about professional athletes who systematically destroy and rebuild their own muscle fibers to achieve their physical goals. I think about the comedian destroying the authority and reputation of the dictator through satire. I think about farmers thinning seedlings, barbers cutting hair, and mechanics disassembling a motor. From the most humble to the grandest scales, destruction makes room for and often feeds creation.

Sun Tzu is an excellent example of the nontoxic Warrior archetype. His legacy as a strategist and philosopher, particularly through his work The Art of War, embodies the Warrior's wisdom, discipline, and focus on mindful action. Sun Tzu emphasized that true strength lies in understanding, preparation, and balance, rather than brute force or aggression. His approach to conflict—favoring strategy, self-control, and knowledge over impulsive action—showcases the divine Warrior's path.

By teaching that "the greatest victory is that which requires no battle," Sun Tzu highlights the Warrior's highest calling: achieving peace and stability through disciplined, ethical strength. His influence continues to resonate as a model of the Warrior archetype focused on accountability, restraint, and deep respect for both opponents and allies.

Another modern example of the Warrior is Dwayne "The Rock" Johnson. Known for his physical strength and discipline, Dwayne Johnson embodies the Warrior's energy. He uses his platform to encourage self-discipline, accountability, and honor, frequently sharing his own struggles and triumphs to motivate others instead of relying on intimidation or aggression to make his might known. He intentionally destroys his own muscle fibers in the gym because he understands the Warrior's drive to destroy needs to be channeled in a beneficial way so that it doesn't become self-destructive or abusive to others.

Intentional destruction is always accompanied by accountability. Accountability is the ability to account for — or give an answer for — one's actions and transactions. Don't confuse this for self-justification or excusing, though. Toxic people who make up excuses, blame, or self-justify their behavior are often trying to avoid negative consequences. You may hear them say things akin to, "The Devil made me do it!" or "If she hadn't made me mad, I wouldn't have done that!" But remember: a soldier without accountability is merely a serial killer.

Growing up, my father reminded my brother and I constantly that no one "makes" us do or feel anything. No one "makes us mad" - we make ourselves mad by taking offense. He taught me the only people to blame for my bad choices are me, myself, and I. When we got in trouble, dad would give us each a turn explaining our sides of the story, calmly focusing us on our own role in the conflict. Little did I know, he was teaching us how to be accountable for our own actions, especially the destructive ones. Ultimately what I learned was that someone who is truly accountable says, "I accept the consequences of my actions because I considered my choices carefully and made my choice on purpose with logic and reason rather than reacting in emotion."

Carl Jung did groundbreaking work on gender energies and the human psyche, which were later expanded by authors like Robert Moore and Douglas Gillette. In their book King, Warrior, Magician, Lover, they described one of the four primary masculine archetypes as: The Warrior. The nontoxic warrior destroys, but like the good sportsman or noble soldier, he follows orders and respects the rules of engagement with accountability. For every archetype, there are two shadows. Moore and Gillette called the dual Shadows of the Warrior "the Sadist" and "the Masochist," but for this book we are going to call them the Abuser and the Defector. The Abuser and the Defector both have problems with accountability. The Abuser is aggressive and refuses to be held accountable for his cruelty. The Defector is ashamed and submits himself to pain or punishment to avoid accountability in himself and others.

It's been my experience that Abuser toxicity most often appears in relation to emotional reactivity. Emotional reactivity is a lack of self-control during highly emotional states, whether positive or negative. This lack of self-discipline when combined with a desire to destroy fuels toxic behaviors like domestic violence or drug abuse. For a less extreme example of the Abuser Warrior type, imagine the child bully who crushes another child's sand castle. Children often let their big emotions like excitement and/or jealousy get the better of their self-control. Destroying the sand castle makes them feel good in that moment. They feel powerful, big, masculine... like a warrior waging an imaginary war.

And what is the first question a caring adult will ask that child? Of course, they ask, "WHY did you do that?" This question, which is so natural to us all, demonstrates the importance of having a reason, a purpose, to destroy. This is accountability in its most basic form. Destruction without accountability is discouraged in both children and adults of all genders in many if not all societies around the world;

however, in some places (looking at you, United States), there is a greater cultural tendency to shrug off male destruction with the "boys will be boys" excuse, stripping the accountability from those moments.

For the most extreme example of the Abuser, consider mass shootings. I know a thing or two about mass murderers, not just because I live in the United States, but also because my elementary school friend almost became one. We were teenagers when he tried to take a duffel bag of his dad's guns to school. His mom intercepted him and called the police. He killed the first officer on the scene and barricaded himself in his room before taking his own life. And all anyone could ask was: why?

Two decades later legislators in my own state make comments about how people who commit gun violence are "simply evil" and that "nothing can be done" - and I ask you: was my friend evil? My friend who cried at the desk behind me during the Columbine shooting, pleading with the teacher to turn it off? My friend who was bullied for not being masculine enough simply because he preferred drawing to sports? Is there really no accountability for the epidemic that is male-enacted homicides and suicides?

Whether you like it or not, mass killings - defined as the killings of three or more persons in one event - are almost exclusively a toxic male phenomenon. (Don't take my word for it. Look it up yourself. A full 97% of mass shooters are men.) Women are just as physically capable of wielding a firearm to destroy random souls, so why don't we? No one seems to ask that question often enough. The answer is **not** that women are inherently better or more moral than men. We aren't. So what then is the difference?

Could it be the results of generations and generations of adults separating destruction from accountability for male children? Think about it. Girls are taught to nurture, to preserve - the opposite of destroying. Meanwhile, boys are ridiculed for nurturing. Think about the types of games, music, and media that are marketed as masculine. How many examples of glorifying meaningless destruction (towards others or oneself) can you count in our cultural elements when you really start looking? That is where the poison is.

Even in sports, if I told you to imagine a coach getting a team of athletes excited by yelling, "We're going to go out there, and we are going to DESTROY THEM!!" and the team all roars together, do you picture a feminine coach and athletes or masculine ones? If you heard someone in a locker room shouting, "NO PAIN NO GAIN," do you imagine a woman or a man? Of course, we imagine men, because it's more masculine to be a destroyer! Fortunately, in sports there is a code of conduct (accountability) which dictates boundaries around the actual amount of destruction being wrought.

Consider a bull-fight. Ernest Hemingway, famed for being one of the most masculine writers of all time, studied the art of bull-fighting with great interest. To Hemingway, the destruction brought on the bull by the matador was an example of "moral violence," which is when a powerful being (the bull) meets their inescapable end with honor and courage in a well-matched fight. It is a form of tragic art that requires a balance of power and respect for death and dying. At the end of a bull fight, a bull might be pardoned for fighting exceptionally, or the bull might die and be sent to the slaughterhouse to become food for the community. Hemingway said that while he always felt sad after a bull-fight, he never felt the disgust that people feel when something is destroyed unfairly or without reason.

Imagine for a moment, the bull-fight without the accountability to traditional rules and respect for death. The matador walks into the stadium with a large firearm instead of a cape and sword. He shoots the bull in the head as soon as he arrives. The carcass is not processed, but rather allowed to rot in the sun while the victor gets paid to take selfies with the creature and people in the community go hungry. This bull-fight would hardly qualify as a fight at all, and certainly would not qualify as tragic art or "moral violence". In fact, this wasteful display would likely evoke strong feelings of disgust. This perfectly illustrates the balance of destruction and accountability.

The Defector Warrior, on the other hand, struggles with immense shame for taking part in destruction or violence, and often feel they deserve pain or punishment in return, sometimes becoming self-destructive or addicted to life-destroying substances. As a result, the Defector will hide from accountability, like the soldier who defects from the army and runs away from giving an account of his actions. The Defector will also refuse to hold others accountable, as he is deeply insecure about his own actions. The problem for the Defector is that until he faces his own demons, he will always be haunted.

The character Sandor Clegane, or The Hound, from Game of Thrones is an outstanding fictional example of the Warrior who struggles with the Defector Shadow. As a boy, Sandor was purposefully burned by his brother Gregor (the Abuser Warrior). For the first half of Game of Thrones, Sandor quietly submits to being the personal bodyguard of Prince Joffrey. Even though Joffrey's cruelty and lack of accountability disgusts Sandor, he believes he deserves a life of violence and misery having been born into and scarred by such a life. By Season 6, Sandor has defected from working for the nobility and hides himself away in a small village where he just wants to stop fighting. But unfortunately, as with many warriors, the war found him again. The Hound was redeemed when he decided to pick back up his axe to fight on behalf of the innocent (Arya), and his redemption was made complete when he faced his monster brother and held HIM accountable by sacrificing both their lives to his greatest fear — fire — in order to break the cycle of meaningless destruction.

Let's pivot back to a nontoxic Warrior: Jesus. As a Baptist preacher's kid, you know I've been itching to bring Jesus into this conversation. You may be asking, "What did Jesus ever destroy?" And the answer is: quite a bit actually. Not least of all, the keys to Death and Hell. You know, it's funny how few of us ask ourselves what that means to destroy the keys to Death and Hell. Maybe I assumed that the keys were destroyed to keep the devils locked away so that Satan couldn't get out. But in my adulthood, I have come to understand that the keys were destroyed so that we all could be free and not have to be locked in with our demons.

Similarly, I've spent a lot of time pondering the scene of Jesus angrily overturning the money-changers' table in the temple courtyard. That was Warrior-Jesus in action, destroying the lies that blessings could be bought or sold. Have you ever noticed in that passage the first thing that is said after Jesus drives them out? He gives an explanation (an account) for exactly why he did what he did, and he doesn't mince words, calling them a den of thieves. Jesus would have known that the most commonly exploited people in these trades were widowed women, and even though he had absolutely nothing to gain, he destroyed the money-changers' whole setup. He drove them out with good reason.

My favorite example of Warrior-Jesus has to be the story of him standing up for the woman caught in the act of adultery as men were trying to stone her. I've returned again and again to that moment in my mind. What was divinely destroyed there? Certainly some egos. But also, old conventions and double standards were placed on the proverbial chopping block. Jesus was actively, purposefully destroying the perspective that it is morally right for some people to subjugate other people — even to death — under the guise of "law". Jesus let the wind out of the sails of their whole party using accountability: "Let he who is without sin cast the first stone." When we see Jesus as one of the masters at nontoxic masculinity, we start to recognize how intentional destruction when aligned with accountability can be both moral and nonviolent.

Consider a modern day example of a Warrior who has been overturning the moneychangers' tables, so to speak, and has confronted the attacks with accountability: Robert F. Kennedy, Jr. If you have never really listened to RFK for whatever reason (maybe because he sounds like Batman, bless him), then you might only know what the talking heads of the pharmaceutical-paid media have to say about him: that he's a "brain-worm infested, anti-vax lunatic" who chops off whale heads and eats roadkill.

How did RFK respond? By being accountable for his actions. He told his stories from his own perspective and said, "Yes, this is what I did, and this is WHY I did it," which is exactly how one takes accountability. He has talked at length about how he learned this nontoxic masculine trait from Alcoholics Anonymous. As often happens with Warriors, they must face a war within their own mind at some point in their lives. For Kennedy, this manifested as his personal war with addiction. He found the way to win the war against self-destruction was through taking accountability and refusing to defect from his larger mission of fighting for a healthy environment for our children, even if it means destroying a system set up by moneychangers in the medical industry.

We honor the spirit of the Warrior across the world, sometimes without even realizing it. For instance, the idea of "the first death" is a theme that resonates through many cultures in terms of initiating children into adulthood, especially boys. From a Christian perspective, once we reach the "age of accountability" we are taught to "crucify ourselves with Christ" and become "reborn as sons of God," with the act of baptism as a ritual demonstrating the death (destruction) of the old self and resurrection of the new self.

Indigenous peoples and non-Christians from all continents have similar rites of passage, which almost always feature intentional self-destruction -- whether it be through literal means, such as tattooing the skin, piercing the body, or ingesting quasi-toxic substances, or through figurative means, such as baptism, bar mitzvahs, or ceremonial dancing. These rites serve as a means to destroy the childish past-self and initiate a new, responsible adult-self who is now accountable to the community.

Why do these rituals persist over time and across cultures? Because all humans have masculine and feminine energies. It is a shared experience. We all feel the urge to destroy, sometimes with reason and sometimes without. We all rely on each other to understand and respect the boundaries of accountability to our communities.

To understand how the Warrior's destructive force can be beneficial on the macro level, let's remember the dismantling of the Berlin Wall. This is a perfect example of how destruction can be both necessary and kind. The intensity of that day is hard to imagine for people who did not live through it, but just to give you an idea: it was reported that many of the 16 million East Berliners finally felt like World War II was over for them, almost thirty years after it had officially ended. There were West Berliners, Russians, and others who were afraid the fall of the wall would cause civil war, chaos, and violence, but they were met with joy and relief instead. It only took weeks for other Eastern European countries to claim their freedoms. Tourism boomed across Europe. Families were reunited. Infrastructure was rebuilt. State-sponsored surveillance systems used for decades to intimidate and persecute East Berliners were removed.

So what accountability went along with the destruction of the Berlin Wall that made it such a success? In 1989-1991, the German government collected, declassified, and published the archives of the Stasi, which were the East German "security force" (read: surveillance, oppression, and torture brigade). The Stasi had attempted to destroy many files via burning or shredding, and the reconstruction of the billions of fragments of paper is still ongoing to this day. When the Stasi archives were opened, anyone could find out the truth about what happened to their family member who disappeared or who was spying on them and why. It was like shining a light onto a mass of cockroaches, and watching them scatter. This was the level of accountability it took to restore trust between neighbors in the newly reunified Germany.

As we close out this first chapter, remember: the Warrior becomes his best self by using his destructive force intentionally, with accountability to his community always. Nontoxic masculinity asserts that we should honor the role of destroyer, and that likewise, the destroyer should account for their actions with great care, truthfulness, and respect for the world around them.

Reflection

Hopefully you're catching on to the idea that masculine demolition energy can be wielded for both good and evil, and that accountability is the key. There's definitely more relating to that message in the pages ahead. But first, take a few minutes to cultivate your own destroyer-of-worlds energy. Here are a few questions to reflect on:

- What in my life am I preserving that I would be better served by destroying?
- When in my life have I destroyed something (relationships included) without purpose or accountability?
- How can I become more balanced in my destructive and creative energies?

Chapter Summary

- Theme: Accountability and Intentional Destruction
- Key to Growth: Integrity and Honor
- Essence: The Warrior archetype embodies strength, decisiveness, and courage. A divine Warrior is proactive and driven by a strong sense of duty to his family and community.
- Pitfall to Avoid: Aggression or destruction without purpose. A Warrior who lacks accountability may become abusive to himself or others.
- Growth Focus: Staying accountable for one's actions, honoring commitments and relationships, and acting with integrity.

2

The Magician

Overview

- **Description:** The Magician is the archetype of power, cleverness, mystery, and story-telling. He understands the hidden forces of the world and seeks to harness them for abundance and healing.
- **Major Conflict:** The Magician faces the challenge of using his powers for good rather than manipulation. He risks becoming either a sly trickster (Illusionist) or an entitled dominator (Sorcerer).
- **Path to Growth:** The Magician grows by using his strengths to empower others, embracing humility and responsibility, and staying connected to the mysteries of life without becoming corrupted.

Stories of the Magician

"The most beautiful thing we can experience is the mysterious. It is the source of all true art and science." – Albert Einstein

We live in a culture that confuses power with control, influence with manipulation. Yet the mightiest leaders throughout history understood that true power comes from serving others, not dominating them. The Magician archetype reminds us that real magic lies in empowering others, not controlling them. The archetype best suited to demonstrate the power aspect of masculinity is the Magician. A true magician holds the power to transform elements, not just perform a sleight of hand for entertainment. The magician at his least toxic, most divine form can channel and combine energy with great precision, resulting in both inspiration and abundance.

A figure in popular modern culture that comes to mind to represent the nontoxic Magician is David Attenborough. As a natural historian and documentarian, Attenborough has revealed the wonders of nature with great power and responsibility. He embodies the Magician's knowledge and reverence for the world, using his talents to inspire awe and environmental stewardship, celebrating rather than exploiting the Earth's abundance. He has undoubtedly pledged himself to the service of our wilderness and all the incredible life that it holds, using his power to draw people into the grand mystery of our planet with his voice and capture their imaginations with storytelling not for personal gain, but for the greater good.

The person who most reminds me of the Magician archetype in my own life is a friend and colleague of my mother's named David Sweaney. From the time I met David, he captivated me. There's just something magical about him. He kind of puts you in mind of a modern-day Merlin, with the white hair but without the beard or pointy hat. His cleverness and ability to tell intriguing stories made him very successful in business and life. When my brother and I were kids and got invited out to dinner with him, he was almost always able to produce some mysterious trinket or gift from his travels as a conversation-starter to delight us. He was able to transform what would have been extremely boring business dinners into hours of entertainment, which is no small feat when you're dealing with ten- and eleven-year olds. Yet every outing with David was somehow dinner AND a show!

This knack for being able to transmute the mundane into the mysterious and magnificent is the gift of the Magician.

Carl Jung actually didn't call this archetype "Magicians" — instead he called them "Alchemists" because they can transform something basic into something valuable and, in essence, attract what they seek to manifest. Jung wrote, "An old alchemist gave the following consolation to one of his disciples: 'No matter how isolated you are and how lonely you feel, if you do your work truly and conscientiously, unknown friends will come and seek you." This has certainly been true for David, who is never at a loss for friends. Magicians are magnetic.

Regardless of what you think of him, Donald Trump is a tremendous example of the Magician, with his own toxic shadow as well as nontoxic potential. He has captured so many people's attention that he has become a household name around the entire world. Think about the amount of wealth and power he has generated for himself and his family. He has a way of story-telling that he calls "the weave" where he cleverly ties a long conversation all the way back around to an earlier story or point in the discussion. This is a way the Magician captivates attention - because the listener is always curious how the conversation will tie back around. You obviously can't win two presidential elections without having some kind of magnetism and keen ability to channel the energy in the room! In fact, he once said, "Without energy, you have nothing." But of course, Donald Trump has a toxic Shadow side, so let's talk about that.

The first Shadow of the Magician is the Illusionist. The Illusionist (or trickster or con artist) recognizes the power that they have to manipulate energy, but their efforts are mostly selfish and involve channeling your economic energy (dollars and cents) into their own pockets. They, too, can change the whole energy of the room, but usually for their own ends, not to promote abundance, but to produce the illusion of scarcity, rivalry, outrage, or supremacy. It is not lost on me that the leaders of the Ku Klux Klan called themselves wizards. Let that sink in.

The second Shadow of the Magician is the Sorcerer. The Sorcerer leans into the idea that he is all-powerful, unstoppable, and superior to less powerful people. Because of this he feels entitled to dominate others as long as it benefits him. We can't talk about domination behavior without discussing a little system called: the Patriarchy. First, though, have you ever heard the joke about the two fish where one fish says, "My, the water sure is nice today!" And the other fish says, "What's water?" Well, that's what it's like to have a conversation about patriarchy.

The patriarchy is not some woke feminist pipe dream. It is a pervasive cultural system that was set up to grant men command over women, children, and "lesser" men in almost all areas of life: physically, economically, socially, psychologically, emotionally, and spiritually. The first rule of the patriarchy is you don't talk about the patriarchy - and I'm not paraphrasing Fight Club as much as I'm paraphrasing bell hooks, who wrote extensively about patriarchy and its effects on both men and women. One of the reasons patriarchy is not pointed out or criticized is because it's widely accepted by both men and women as "the natural order." And we aren't supposed to ever question "the natural order," right?

Unfortunately the most toxic tenant of patriarchy is that men are encouraged to exercise domination against themselves and others, especially women, children, and non-patriarchy-conforming ("inferior") people, to prove their toxic masculine superiority. To exercise domination against themselves, boys are required by the patriarchy to repress their emotional selves, to control their "feminine" emotions (sadness, caring, adoration, cheer, anxiety, etc.) and only exert their "masculine" emotions (indifference, competitiveness, rowdiness, anger, etc.) in order to gain the approval or attention of their parents and peers.

There's a nontoxic Magician named Richie Reseda who read bell hooks's work while in prison. Raised in Los Angeles, Richie had a front row seat to toxic masculinity and one of the patriarchy's biggest underminers of men, but especially men of color: the school-to-prison pipeline. At age 19 he was sentenced to 10 years in state prison for a non-violent crime. But instead of becoming more deviant or bitter, Reseda realized the power of words. Now he speaks truth to power all over the country to help rehabilitate criminals from their toxic masculinity by teaching them to dismantle their inner patriarchy and become open to connecting and being vulnerable without shame or domination.

To see how the Magician gets corrupted, let's examine the story where Jesus fasts in the wilderness for forty days and is tempted by Lucifer. I always found this story to be ridiculous, myself. Some of you haven't heard this story, so I'll paraphrase: after Jesus had fasted for 40 days in the wilderness, the Devil appears and tempts Jesus to show off his magical powers. First he says: turn this stone into bread. Jesus declines. Then he dares Jesus to throw himself off the temple to let the angels save him. Decline. Finally he takes him to the top of a mountain and says: you can have all this if you just bow to me. Of course this is where the most famous version of the "Not today, Satan" meme originated.

The ridiculous parts of this story to me were never the responses of Jesus but the offers of Satan. Why is he tempting Jesus to eat when my dude already fasted forty days and is clearly an expert in food restriction? And then to follow "magic this rock into bread" with "throw yourself off this building" was a real twist. Why would you ask a savior to prove he could be saved? And then his third attempt is essentially, "Bow to me and I'll promise you all this land and stuff". But again, what is the point? Why would Jesus want land or wealth when literally all he did was go around preaching for people to give their money to the poor? It doesn't make sense. As a kid, I thought that the Devil was certainly a clown for choosing those things in an attempt to trick anyone, Jesus least of all.

However, understanding this episode of Jesus's life as a parable for nontoxic masculinity reveals the hidden truth of the story, which is: it's all about power. Satan tempts Jesus to be irresponsible with his power in three very distinct ways: by self-serving, by dominating, and by false entitlement. These are the three ways that masculine power becomes corrupt.

The most basic level of power corruption is self-serving Trickster behavior, that is using your power to put your needs and desires ahead of others' welfare. Turning stones into bread is like taking a bribe. When someone accepts a bribe, they usually do so in exchange for manipulating some outcome from unfavorable (stone) to favorable (bread) for their own benefit, without regard for others.

Next in the parable, when Satan tempts Jesus to throw himself from a cliff and call angels to save him, what he's doing is tempting Jesus to take command of the angels from a place of superiority. He's tempting Jesus to use his power to dominate others' time and attention like the Sorcerer Shadow. He probably recognized that Jesus wouldn't be easily tempted to violently dominate others, so the power play Satan presented was "harmless" but still dominating.

When elements of shame, self-doubt, and insecurity are introduced, the dominating magician might exert force in order to try to prove himself as worthy or competent, not just powerful. After the first failed attempt at temptation, Satan begins quoting scripture as a strategy for invoking that insecurity needed to push Jesus into a corruption of his power. "If you are the Son of God," the Devil taunted, just begging for Jesus to prove himself. As we know, he didn't fall for it, but think about how many would fall for a similar "if you were a real man" setup. His wisdom allowed him to escape the snare of corruption.

The final step up the ladder of corruption and into the Sorcerer Shadow is false entitlement. False entitlement is when a person believes they are deserving of power or that they are owed power when they have not actually earned the power, wealth, or respect that they desire. To entitle someone is to grant them the title (power) over some place, person, position or object. Not always but many times, false entitlement is coupled with fraud or theft of some kind. Historically, we can see how lands (and human beings) were stolen from one group and entitled to another group, over and over.

In the parable's context, Satan very literally tried to hand over the title of all the kingdoms in all the Earth to Jesus if he would agree to… bend the knee. Seriously, the original word for "worship" used by Satan in his request meant "to kiss the hand." He wanted to entitle Jesus, to legitimize him as the one true king of all Westeros - I mean, Judea. However, Jesus recognized that if he accepted, it would be a false entitlement, a long con, a title which neither he deserved nor was Satan sanctioned to offer him. Thus, he replied by saying: thanks, but no thanks - that title belongs to the Almighty God. He rejected the temptation to become corrupted.

Much power originates from the knowing of secrets. We have probably all heard children say the phrase: "I know something you don't know." This is a very low-level example of dominating behaviors, but it's a great example because we can all relate to it. The power the dominating child holds is in the secret they know, but it's also in the curiosity of others who want to know the same secret. Nothing takes the wind out of a dominator's sails quite like replying with, "I don't care." Because if you don't want to know the secret, then the person flaunting the secret does not hold much power over you or your attention.

Most dominating is either attention-seeking or self-proving behavior, so it's equally important to consider the opposite of these two things. It's my humble opinion that the opposite of attention-seeking is connection-seeking. Attention seekers say, "Look at me! Look at what only I know how to do! I have the secret!" By contrast, connection seekers say, "Look at us. Look what we can accomplish together. We can exchange our secrets to make us both better." The emphasis changes from withholding secrets to sharing them, creating connection and intimacy, and breaking down the idea that the person holding the secret is somehow superior to the one who is not.

A man who does not feel the need to prove himself usually has a solid sense of self worth and inner power (self esteem) as well as strong connections to others. The self-proving dominator, however, lacks the self-worth and self-esteem required to be vulnerable and form intimate bonds with others. They fear being "found out" as inferior in some way. In order for these toxic Magicians to change, they must embrace the wisdom that superiority-versus-inferiority is an illusion we've been conditioned to believe. A self-administered dose of humility is sometimes required, but a boost of pride in oneself might also be needed. The balance point is understanding that all people, including ourselves, are both good and bad and neither superior nor inferior. We all deserve certain fundamental rights, and we all have basic needs. We all just want to be ourselves.

The nontoxic Magician sees domination for what it is: control that has been equated to power. They recognize that they have nothing to prove, and they value intimate bonds with others, based on partnership and mutual respect. Like Jesus refusing to throw himself off the building to "make" the angels come save him, the nontoxic Magician is not interested in wasting others' time and effort to demonstrate his power over them. They don't fall into the trap of thinking that they are entitled to be served by others and instead, seek to serve others and become servant-leaders (an idea discussed at large by John Maxwell and enacted with much grace by Richie Reseda and others.)

The abusive husband might have many faces - the drunk, the rager, the liar, the cheater, the tyrant, the saboteur - but underlying all the types of abuse is a fundamental belief that the person enacting the abuse is entitled to do so, oftentimes justified by the fact that their significant other isn't meeting their needs. This is something the Greeks called: Hubris.

Hubris, which we have modernly equated with pride or arrogance, used to be a word that was much harsher in meaning, more like a violent overpowering or violation of another. Philosophers like Aristotle emphasized that hubris was not merely aggression but a willful disregard for the dignity of others. It stemmed from an overinflated sense of superiority. Someone who acted with hubris was basically assuming entitlement of something that belonged to God - like another human being. You can probably guess why this word was toned down to mean "pride" over time. I'm sure it was a particularly troublesome definition to grapple with during the mass hubris of the age of Chattel Slavery. But certainly even in today's world, the true definition of hubris is a hard pill to swallow for people who regularly participate in war and tolerate unusual amounts of gun violence.

The antidote to hubris and the opposite of false entitlement is divine deference, which is the wisdom that no one and nothing truly belongs to any individual, but that we all ultimately belong to God. From ashes to ashes - our lives and all our ideas of ownership and who-is-entitled-to-what are temporary. When I recognize that all beings belong to God and that only God can judge them, I no longer feel entitled to hold judgment, project superiority, or inflict control or suffering upon them. This ideology can be expressed in a less religious context by considering the belief in "inalienable rights" of life, liberty and the pursuit of happiness. When we dominate or control others, we are taking away their inalienable rights in one way or another. We are acting in hubris. That is the poison.

The nontoxic Magician believes that God gives and God takes away, that rain falls on both the just and unjust, and that they are not entitled to exert judgment or violent force against others, as we are all equal and beloved in the sight of God. The nontoxic Magician believes that empowering others does not diminish his own power, that power belongs to the people, and that domination of other people's power over their lives, liberties, and pursuits of happiness is morally corrosive and hubristic.

Reflection

That's right — "Y'er a wizard, 'Arry!" I hope this chapter helped you understand and appreciate your divine Magician energy a little bit more. Before we move onto the Kings, take a moment to reflect on your own relationship to power:

- In what ways have you used your power to serve only yourself? In what ways have you used power to serve others?

- How can you be more responsible with your power? Are there areas in your life where you have been employing control tactics instead of respecting God's will (divine deference)?
- How has the patriarchy or other social institutions (i.e. religion, economy, media) influenced your ideas about who should and should not have power in your daily life?

Chapter Summary

- Theme: Power and Energy
- Key to Growth: Responsibility and Divine Deference
- Essence: The Magician represents mystery, production, alchemy, and transformation. He has the power to channel energy and turn words into gold.
- Pitfall to Avoid: Manipulation or misuse of power for personal gain; entitlement and hubris.
- Growth Focus: Using power ethically, valuing connection and relinquishing superiority with divine deference, and embracing the responsibility of one's influence.

The King

Overview

- **Description:** The King represents leadership, respect, and order. He is the archetype of authority and has the ability to create structure and stability.
- **Major Conflict:** The King struggles with the balance between control and respect. He risks becoming either a control freak (Tyrant) or an indulgent people pleaser (Puppet).
- **Path to Growth:** The King becomes his best self by leading with trustworthiness, fostering collaboration and respect, and using his strengths to create a just and harmonious kingdom.

Stories of the King

"The painful secret of gods and kings is that men are free."
-Jean-Paul Sartre

We've talked about the Warriors.
We've talked about the Magicians.
Now, we talk about the Kings.

Too often we conflate authority with authoritarianism and leadership with dominance. Yet the most exceptional leaders throughout history understood that true authority comes not from force, but from trust. The King archetype reminds us that real power lies in respecting others, not ruling over them. The King archetype demonstrates the masculine relationships to leadership, authority, and respect. The biggest strength of the King is that he can bring order to chaos and inspire loyalty.

Where Donald Trump is a Magician, Bernie Sanders is a King. This is not a political statement — it's an observation on their strengths and struggles. Whether you love or loathe President Trump, you cannot convince me that his gift is bringing order to chaos or inspiring deep loyalty. If anything, he's really excellent at creating controlled-chaos, but again, in the way of smoke-and-mirrors like the Magician. If you think his followers are super loyal, you should know as soon as he slid the Epstein Files back in the lock-box, half his base turned on him!

By contrast, if you put your personal feelings about Senator Sanders aside, we can all admit he is the definition of a community organizer with an extremely loyal following, to the point that he is lionized among progressives. So what exactly is it that made so many people in 2016 and again in 2020 "Feel the Bern"? We craved leadership whom we could trust to build a better system (order), not built on power, secrecy, and control, but on empowering the people, telling the truth, and restoring moral authority to a corrupt government.

Some say a picture is worth a thousand words, and one of the most compelling photos I've ever seen was of a Bernie Sanders rally at Queensbridge Park, New York City in October of 2019. The crowd was absolutely massive! The trait that gives Bernie his appeal is not production value, it's trustworthiness. Especially before 2020, Sanders was considered one of the only politicians to not be a sell-out to lobbying groups and super-PACs, and he had a long record of experience that made him the prime authority on government of the people, by the people.

The most King-oriented man in my own life is my step-father Lanny Dunn, or "Big Daddy" as his grandchildren call him. His knack for systems-thinking (order) brought him from being a family farm-hand to having a small empire of car dealerships, body shops, and service centers. His customers and employees are a loyal bunch, mostly because they know they can trust Lanny to not only be knowledgeable about his products but also to always be fair and honest. While car salesmen tend to have a reputation for being pushy or manipulative, Lanny makes sales with ease, not force, and respects the customer decisions to buy whenever they're ready. As a result of his success, he has won dozens of awards in his industry. Fun fact: when you're among the best Toyota dealers in the world, the company awards you with different pieces of historically accurate Samurai armor! That's why if you ever walk into Lanny's office, you'll see he has both a Samurai sword and helmet on display. Awards fit for a King!

Remember in the last chapter that we discussed how power and control are two different things, but the toxic Magician confuses the two? Almost exactly the same thing applies in this chapter with the concept of authority and force. Jungian psychologists describe the archetypal King as having two toxic Shadows: Tyrant and Puppet. The toxic Tyrant King thinks that to gain authority he must evoke fear through harsh punishment and forceful discipline of others. That is just not true! Similarly, the toxic Puppet King thinks his authority comes from being permissive and seeking to please and be pleased. This is equally false!

Nontoxic Kings understand that authority comes from trust, not titles. Did you know the word "authority" is related to the words "author" and "authentic"? In fact, in Middle English the word "authority" meant "some person or written passage with the capacity to inspire trust". Before that, in Latin, it meant "trusted advice." The concept of a person as "an authority figure" originally reflected the trustworthiness of that person to help solve a problem with wisdom and fairness. The word "trust" itself comes from Old Norse and means "to rely on to make strong and safe".

In Ancient Rome, there were village mediators who were presented with problems between villagers and would find a solution, many times a past solution written in the local history that was proven to work and that respected all persons involved, and those mediators were called: the authorities. We still apply this term today to officers of the law who are trusted to settle disputes and help solve community problems. The word "respect" simply means "to consider another's thoughts and feelings before speaking or acting in a way that will affect them". Respect builds trust, and trust builds authority.

When toxicity creeps in, the role of the so-called authorities becomes poisoned with distrust, disrespect, and corrupt behavior - sometimes to the extent of dehumanization of others. You'll notice that in some communities where policing was implemented more like a form of slave patrol, they don't refer to police as "the authorities" because the trust and respect are gone, and instead you'll hear police referred to as "law enforcement," which says the word 'force' right there in it. In the book of Mark, he describes Jesus as amazing people with his teachings "because he taught them as one who had authority, not as the teachers of the law" (Mark 1:22). Even back then, people understood that simply knowing and enforcing the law as well as the Pharisees did was not enough to grant them the actual authority that comes with respect and trust.

Let's take a look at the most obvious example of a King from the Old Testament: King Solomon. You may remember this story from Sunday School, but it is worth revisiting. In the first Book of Kings, there is a story that has become known as "The Judgment of Solomon" in which two mothers who had both given birth recently appeared before the king to solve a dispute about the children. During the night, one of the infants had died and one mother, who switched her dead baby for the live one, was claiming the live baby was her own. Solomon orders his sword be brought to cut the living child into two parts to give one part to each woman. The false mother agreed to this arrangement. The true mother cried before the king that she would rather the other woman take her child than see the child harmed. Of course, Solomon did not cut the baby in two. He gave the baby back to the mother who clearly cared most for the life of the child.

What first stands out to me about this story is that the king held an audience with these two women in the first place. Imagine a toxic King in the same position. A Tyrant would have easily dismissed this situation entirely or killed all three subjects just to stop them from wailing; a Puppet would have said, "Just give the child to the loudest woman so that she won't smear my name to my subjects." But Solomon flexed his respect for his female subjects and brought them into his court to hear their case. We know that Solomon was deeply respectful because he had to consider how the true mother must feel about her child in order to make his choice. His consideration of others' thoughts and feelings led him to a just decision.

My own great-uncle Leonard Lawson showed me the respectfulness of a true King. Not only did he loudly and proudly respect the women in his life, but he did so in an era where misogyny was the norm, especially of those working in his industry of construction. He cherished his mother, his sisters, and his wife, who was also his high school sweetheart, by the way. Later on, when he had nieces and nephews and great-nieces and great-nephews, he would sit with us for hours, listening to our stories and counseling us on our problems, often with a wink and a half-grin. He would take us fishing and laugh proudly if we young folks brought in a bigger catch than the grown folks. By that time he was a wealthy and powerful business owner, but to watch him engage with my brother, cousins, and I so respectfully and attentively, you would have thought we were the most important things on his to-do list. This deep respect is a hallmark of the King and inspires great loyalty.

By contrast, the toxic King is disrespectful, untrustworthy, and judgmental. Think about the Tyrant and Puppet Kings - actual monarchs - who fit that description. What Tyrants and Puppet Kings have in common is they disrespect, lie, and judge, but the Tyrant does so externally, and the Puppet does so internally. The Tyrant disrespects others, lies to others, and/or judges others without mercy. The Puppet disrespects himself, he lies to himself, he judges himself without mercy. The toxic King is often indulgent and materialistic, which are disrespectful sins at their core because the gluttonous King is not respecting the feelings of the hungry peasant, nor is the greedy King respecting the poor. They lie and punish others, even unto death, in accordance with their own interest, because who can stop them? And they believe the royal "because I said so" proves their authority.

Consider how the revered leader Sitting Bull displayed the opposite of the Tyrant or Puppet Kings, through his steadfast authority, respect and discernment, and an unwavering commitment to protecting his people's sovereignty, freedom, and way of life. Sitting Bull's leadership extended beyond warfare; he held a deep spiritual authority and loyalty among his people. His visions and counsel guided key decisions, and he balanced strength with profound respect for the Lakota's cultural values. His refusal to compromise with U.S. government's demands and his role in defending his people's land and traditions reflect the King's dedication to justice and unwillingness to trade his people's trust for pleasing any politician. Sitting Bull led with a focus on collective well-being and deep respect, prioritizing the long-term interests of his people over personal gain or revenge against his enemies.

The King's relationship with liberty reveals their growth and maturity as a leader. A healthy King respects and upholds liberty, understanding that true leadership is not about control, but about empowering others to thrive within a framework of stability and justice. The King archetype embodies the principle of governance, which inherently involves balancing order and freedom. Liberty represents the freedom of individuals to live, think, and act autonomously within the structure established by the King. Without liberty, the King risks descending into tyranny and losing the respect and trust of those he leads. Liberty ensures that the King's authority is grounded in mutual respect rather than fear. Without sufficient freedoms, the King risks stirring a rebellion. King Solomon, Sitting Bull, and Bernie Sanders all understood this concept.

But allowing people to get away with or take whatever liberties they want is equally toxic. For an example of how favoritism can create this toxic environment for a Puppet King, we can look at King David, Solomon's father, in the book of Second Samuel. David had several sons by different women, and his household had complex family dynamics, but his son Absalom was said to be the most handsome and well-liked by the people. Another of David's sons, Amnon, raped David's daughter, who was Absalom's sister. However, because Amnon was David's heir, David failed to take decisive action to punish him, which angered Absalom. In response to David's inaction, Absalom took justice into his own hands, killing his half-brother.

Instead of disciplining Absalom, David showed him leniency and allowed him to return from exile, signaling favoritism toward him despite the murder. Absalom exploited this liberty as well as his own popularity and began to plot against David's authority, eventually leading a rebellion to seize the throne. Absalom's rebellion forced David to flee Jerusalem, plunging the kingdom into chaos and civil war. The conflict ended tragically with Absalom's death at the hand of David's most trusted general Joab, who had been instructed to spare Absalom's life, but feared the king would let his emotional bias impact his discernment again. Joab decided that taking matters into his own hands and leaving David heartbroken and undermined at once was better than opening the kingdom to a future second rebellion.

David's actions underscore his internal conflict as both a father and a King. His personal desire to please and cater to Absalom clouded his judgment, and his inability to reconcile his roles as a parent and King contributed to the tragedy. While David sought to preserve Absalom's life, his favoritism and lack of impartiality ultimately weakened his position as a trusted authority and led to a cascade of events that destabilized his rule.

The primary conflict of Kings is the temptation to consider themselves "above the law." Toxic Kings will act as if their word IS law or as if laws should not apply to them. Sometimes toxic Kings will impose harsh rules upon themselves and hold themselves to an often unachievable standard - this too is a King malfunction. Sometimes they will "take liberties" - isn't that an interesting turn of phrase knowing now that respecting liberty is the cornerstone of a nontoxic King? All of these are ego issues.

The ego is an interesting creature. Carl Jung described it as a small but fierce part of our overall psyches that rules over the subconscious mind by creating belief systems around "who we are" and simultaneously suppressing uncomfortable truths about our identity. When the ego completely rejects uncomfortable truths about ourselves, it creates our "shadow self" that must be confronted in order to self-actualize. To the King, the most uncomfortable truth is that he is not special or wholly unique. He is as ordinary as any subject and, therefore, is not above the law.

Just for giggles, if you know a King, try asking them why they think they are so special. It'll strike a nerve with their inner Tyrant every time. It is deeply uncomfortable for them to admit that they are ordinary because they believe that ordinary people have to follow the rules that extraordinary people get to make and also ignore. The ego becomes inflated by flatterers, by self-focus, by arrogance and grandiosity. However, the ego can become integrated by alignment with the higher self and divine masculinity.

To align your ego with your higher self, start by considering the purpose of the King: to create order that allows people around them to thrive. Maybe you are someone who has naturally attracted loyal followers who seek your direction. This is a sign that you hold King energy. It's very tempting to think: People are drawn to me because there is just something unique and special about me. That kind of thinking feeds the shadow of the ego by suppressing the uncomfortable truth that we are all ordinary. Instead, understand the higher truth that even ordinary people have special gifts, and the gift of the King is the ability to make thoughtful decisions that provide a benevolent structure for all his subjects to exist in harmony.

Consider the example of Henry Ford, King of the American auto industry. Ford was not wholly nontoxic (who is?) and was often referred to as a Tyrant or dictator for his ruthless business dealings. However, his legacy was in the order he created: the assembly line. Ford revolutionized the entire auto industry by standardizing car production and creating the assembly line process for their manufacturing. This structure that he created made it possible for the average American to afford an automobile. Additionally Ford paid his workers remarkably well for the time - more than twice the average wage for manufacturing workers in 1914.

I bet you've heard plenty about Henry Ford and the success of his assembly line idea, but maybe you haven't heard about his greatest failure: Fordlandia. In true King fashion, Henry Ford purchased 2.5 million acres of the Amazon Rainforest in Brazil with the goal of creating a utopian industrial colony of America in a place where rubber could be produced for American tires. He set up housing, schools, hospitals, a golf course, and American-style restaurants on property, and he also set up some strict rules: no alcohol, no tobacco, no single women, no music, no dancing, and absolutely NO SIESTAS. (Gasp!) These strict rules created the perfect environment for black market activity and secret jungle parties to emerge.

Not only that, but Ford failed to listen to local authorities on how to best grow the rubber trees, which led to pest, disease, and crop failure. Within two years of purchasing the property and setting up the infrastructure, Ford's little kingdom came crashing down when workers rioted until the Brazilian National Guard showed up. In case you're curious, there are still ruins of Fordlandia standing today and plenty of pictures online, as it still lays abandoned despite being sold back to the government of Brazil for a fraction of the original price in 1945.

So what made Henry Ford such a success on one hand and such an abject failure on the other? Where he was successful, he gained trust through respect from a place of empathy. Where he failed, he tried to force compliance through rules from a place of ego. He forced Brazilian workers to eat American food, work American hours, and plant rubber trees American-style (mono-cropped and close together) because his ego was so large that he felt ordained to "civilize" the people of Fordlandia and do things HIS way.

Consider how absurd it is to think you know better how to live and operate in a place than the people who have lived hundreds of years in that place. That's one of the uncomfortable truths that every colonizer suppresses with their egos - that they rarely know better than indigenous peoples about how to create success in a vastly different environment. They inflate their egos by thinking that because they have experienced success in one place, then they are clearly special and thus must travel to other places to spread specialness to all the presumably un-special peoples. The hard truth for Kings like Ford is: men are free. Trying to establish order through force is only ever going to end in frustration.

True nontoxic authority is gained neither through might nor through right, but through insight. To have insight and discernment, Kings must be willing to consider the thoughts, feelings, and lived experiences of others (respect) while remaining trustworthy through their integrity, discernment, and dedication to liberty and justice for all. Only then can the true King create a magnificent and harmonious kingdom.

Reflection

Long live the King! I hope you enjoyed this chapter and are looking forward to the next one, but before we take a walk down lovers' lane, let's take a moment for a few questions for His Royal Highness (you):

- Where have you enforced overly strict rules in your own life or relationships? How can you repair respect and trust in those situations?
- When have you let your ego get a little too inflated or bruised? How can you confront your shadow by examining uncomfortable truths?

- Who in your life are you actively disrespecting (a.k.a. not considering their thoughts and feelings before making decisions that impact them)?

Chapter Summary
- Theme: Authority and Order
- Key to Growth: Trust and Respect
- Essence: The King is the archetype of trustworthiness, fairness, and compassionate discernment. He upholds order and inspires loyalty.
- Pitfall to Avoid: Pride and punishment
- Growth Focus: Demonstrating authority through integrity, respecting the dignity and liberty of others, and valuing trust-through-respect over compliance-through-discipline.

4

The Lover

Overview

- **Description:** The Lover embodies passion and connection. He is the archetype of sensuality, appreciation, and the pursuit of beauty.
- **Major Conflict:** The Lover faces the challenge of balancing his passions with his expectations and setting boundaries. He risks becoming either love-addicted (Hedonist) or emotionally cut off and unforgiving (Hermit).
- **Path to Growth:** The Lover grows by cultivating deep, meaningful relationships, appreciating the beauty in life, and expressing his passions in healthy, creative and compassionate ways.

Stories of the Lover

"Love does not consist in gazing at each other, but in looking outward together in the same direction." – Antoine de Saint-Exupery

Modern culture tells men their positive emotions make them weak, that expressing love and appreciating beauty makes them

"SIMPS." Yet the greatest leaders, artists, and change-makers throughout history have been men who dared to love deeply and passionately. The Lover archetype reminds us that passion isn't weakness — it's power channeled through connection. This aspect of masculine energy is one of the most misunderstood, so let's start with square one: what is love? (Baby, don't hurt me... sorry, couldn't resist.) In her book "All About Love" bell hooks defined love as: "a combination of care, commitment, knowledge, responsibility, respect and trust."

Growing up, I had a youth pastor named Gary Alley who might have read bell hooks, honestly, because he knew all about love. Maybe you think all youth pastors are toxic creeps, but Gary was (and still is) a genuinely caring, knowledgeable, committed, trustworthy, responsible, and respectful man of God — just like the definition above. He deeply loved his community, offering himself in service to whomever had a need. Multiple days every week, he spent encouraging, loving, and helping people all around town, including hosting a Thursday night Bible study at his house where he and his wife fed up to two dozen teenagers, both literally and spiritually.

One night at Bible study, we had been discussing "spiritual gifts," and I asked Gary what he thought my gift was, and he replied: LOVE. I was instantly confused. Love? How was love a gift? Moreover, can I trade up for prophecy because that seems like a lot cooler gift than love? Gary half-grinned. Then he said something that stuck with me forever: "You're blessed to have the same gift as Mother Teresa." I had never thought about love as a super power until that moment.

But the real reason that I'm including Gary here with the Lover archetype and not with the Sage (because clearly, he was wise) is that what struck me most in my many years of knowing and serving alongside him was his deep reverence for beauty. Every spring I could find him out in the yard with a big floppy sun hat planting flowers so that his wife and he could have something beautiful to look at from their office and quilting room windows. He made jokes about his own singing voice, but he played guitar and led us in worship songs and hymns multiple times a week because he loved the beauty of our harmonies, which often moved him to tears. When we went on mission trips together, sometimes I'd catch him gazing in wonder at the beauty of creation, no doubt praying thanksgivings with his eyes open. This appreciation for beauty is the hallmark of the Lover.

Society generally defines love as "passionate devotion," but the Lover has to learn where to draw the line between love and passion. Whole wars have been fought in the name of passionate devotion. Is a "crime of passion" really more morally acceptable to us than a premeditated crime? Does a relentless pursuit of passion justify neglecting or abusing ourselves, family, or communities? Song lyrics of John Mayer ring in my head, "Love ain't a crutch, it ain't an excuse. No you can't get through love on just a pile of IOUs. Love ain't a drug, despite what you've heard. Yeah, love ain't a thing. Love is a verb."

Jungian psychologists said the Lover archetype has two possible Shadows: the addicted Lover (Hedonist) or the impotent Lover (Hermit). Both of these toxic Lover types struggle with one thing: boundaries. The addicted Lover sets too few boundaries. The impotent Lover sets too many. The nontoxic Lover sets just the right amount of boundaries. What many people fail to understand is that setting boundaries requires learning how to reject judiciously.

The toxic Hedonist Lover energy can manifest in many ways, but typically they treat love like a drug. They may or may not engage in other addiction behaviors (i.e. substance abuse, work addiction, etc.), but typically there are patterns of using someone or thing to avoid or numb pain. The Hedonist Lover possesses unbounded love - love that knows no healthy boundaries. This shouldn't be confused with unconditional love, because even the Hedonist Lover sets conditions or expectations on their love objects.

We can better understand unbounded love by examining a familiar character: Don Juan. The story of Don Juan is that he was a wealthy man who traveled about, putting on all manner of disguises to seduce women of all ages and stations until his lust turned to violence and resulted in judgement. Was Don Juan a Lover? Yes. Was he passionately devoted to his mission of seducing women? Yes. Could you say he was addicted to love? Yes. Could you say that his love knew no bound-aries? Yes. However, can we say he loved unconditionally? Absolutely not. Is he a toxic or nontoxic masculine figure? I don't have to an-swer that for you. You know Don Juan to be toxic. He was the origi-nal love-em-and-leave-em, a classic addicted Lover who used love for selfish pleasure.

The Hermit Lover has the exact opposite problem with bound-aries: they set way too many. They box themselves in and/or block others out. The most common reason for too many boundaries is fear and insecurity. Usually, the toxic Hermit Lover is afraid their love ob-ject will reject or abandon them, but sometimes they fear hurting or violating their love object. Other times they fear how they will be per-ceived by society. There's almost always some element of fear hold-ing back the impotent Lover, and what do we do when we are afraid? We put up fences and walls to protect ourselves, stifling our own lov-ing energy. The Bible claims that "perfect love casts out all fear." This should be noted by Hermit Lovers.

Instead of looking at a religious or fictional example of the Lover, let's look at a historic example: Frederick Douglass. I know, probably not who you expected me to pick, but Frederick Douglass was quite the Lover. As an infant his mother was taken from him, but for a short time, he was able to stay with his maternal grandmother Bet-sey Bailey who instilled love into him as a boy before he was sent out to work on the plantations. As a young man, he found favor with his slaveowner's daughter, who showed him compassion, warmth, and kindness and also her aunt, who taught him the alphabet.

Douglass was said to have been highly attractive and naturally charming. He was passionately devoted to many causes throughout his life, from the abolition of slavery to women's rights to promoting literacy and education for all. His writings and speeches were infused with fiery appeals to emotion, which Elizabeth Cady Stanton de-scribed as "burning eloquence."

But did you know his first wife Anna Murray, a free black woman who worked as a housekeeper in Baltimore, loved Douglass so much she used her savings plus donations raised by two English activists, the Robinson sisters, to help him escape slavery? Murray and Douglass then married and had five children together, and Murray largely ignored rumors of Douglass's mistresses and flirtations, even though he traveled often and invited Julia Griffiths (a British abolitionist) to move in with them for some time, which caused quite a scandal. Regardless, Anna remained a dutiful and practical wife until she died.

After Anna passed away, Douglass married Helen Pitts who was 20 years younger, much more well-connected, and white, to beat it all. The community scorned them from all sides, including Douglass's own children, and Douglass just laughed and said: "This proves I am impartial. My first wife was the color of my mother and the second, the color of my father." After Douglass died, it was Pitts who continued to fight for his legacy to be memorialized, showing how his love crossed the boundaries of not only race and social status but also of life and death.

Too often the Lover archetype is made to feel shame for his ability to love and be loved. He is too often falsely accused of hedonism. Multiple times in his life, Frederick Douglass was scorned or shamed over his lovers. If the word "SIMP" had existed, he would have been called that. He was accused of extramarital affairs in the press, with no substantial evidence, and rejected every claim as false. Interestingly, all the women in Douglass's life stood by him, describing him as caring and kind, never having taken advantage. Rather than become one of the toxic versions of the Lover, Douglass forgave those who scorned him and continued to love and be loved. In fact, toward the end of his life Douglass wrote about forgiving his own enslaver, something which upset some of his friends and fellow activists, but Douglass understood the role of the Lover: to find those who can be passionate with you and release expectations through forgiveness.

What happens when the Lover doesn't understand the assignment? The Hedonist Lover uses his gifts of attraction to seek pleasure and numb heartache, often at others' expense. If you're on BookTok, you know the Hedonistic Lover as: the Rake. We've already talked about Don Juan, who was certainly a picture of the Hedonist Lover. But the opposite side of the toxic coin is the Hermit. The Hermit Lover internalizes shame or pain around loving and decides to just not love at all. For a Lover to not be loved, they must isolate themselves and practice absolute rejection of self and others. Otherwise they will be loved (now I'm singing Maroon 5, but I digress).

Many times toxic Lovers have a dysfunctional relationship with loving and intimacy in large part because their passionate nature leads them to build up romantic expectations and idealistic fantasies of others. These expectations are rarely met in reality, which launches toxic Lovers into chasing the fantasy (Hedonist) or abandoning love in disappointment and bitterness (Hermit). This tendency to hold high expectations can also be a double-edged sword for the Lover. They may internalize their failure to realize a love that exceeds their expectations as a character flaw or unworthiness of sorts. They may dwell on "the one who got away" and be consumed by melancholy. This is an example of the unhealed Lover using their own passionate nature to punish themselves, and sometimes it is downright dramatic. Sorry, boys.

So then what does a Lover need to confront in his Shadow to help him become his highest self? He must learn how to release his expectations. Lovers tend toward fantasies of "soul mates" who will share their passionate devotions. They create a belief around what they expect from their "ideal" or "one true love" and justify hedonistic or overly judgmental behavior as simply still searching for "the one" or "having high standards." Consider Harry Styles here or even Taylor Swift, for a feminine example. Releasing expectations means unwinding the belief that there is an "ideal person" before that lie becomes your idol. The way to dismantle expectation is through examining your assumptions and beliefs so that you can find grace, freedom, and forgiveness. Start by asking yourself: why do I expect so much?

In The Mastery of Love, by Don Miguel Ruiz, he writes about how we've all been "domesticated" by our upbringing to believe certain ways or assume certain things. When we enter into relationships, we practice the art of loving by realizing that none of what our partners say or do is personal, but only a product of their beliefs and assumptions and dreams, which may be different than our own, and that is ok. We can forgive them and offer them grace, knowing most people are simply doing their best. Ruiz writes, "If you decide to be with a person, don't try to change anything about her. Just like your dog or your cat, let her be who she is. She has the right to be who she is." By releasing expectations and letting your lovers be fully themselves, you begin to unlock the divine Lover archetype.

Be careful not to confuse forgiving and releasing expectations for holding no boundaries. Always saying "yes" to every request and never saying "no" or rejecting requests from your beloved is indulgent and can lead to codependent relationships between Lovers and the people they love. Setting boundaries can also be called "managing expectations" because really, the codependent beloved has unrealistic expectations of her Lover. Since the Lover is naturally very open to experience, they often say "yes" to most things right away! Then, their partners begin to expect too much from them, usually ending in suffering.

The uncomfortable truth the Lover must confront is: love is never earned nor bought, it is only ever freely given as a gift. It can be withdrawn or lost but never truly becomes unavailable when you're open to loving another. Ever heard that song lyric, "I can't make you love me if you don't"? That's part of the uncomfortable truth of the Lover. When the Lover accepts this truth, his higher self can confront partners with unrealistic expectations and demands by saying, "I love you, but no." Many unhealed Lovers are afraid if they set these boundaries, their partner will abandon them, and that makes them feel uncertainty and doubt (negative expectations). But remember Don Miguel Ruiz's words: "If one person doesn't love you, someone else will love you."

Keanu Reeves is a beautiful modern example of the Lover who leans toward the Hermit shadow but knows how to find redemption in both releasing expectations and drawing boundaries. In early adulthood, Keanu experienced the still birth of his first child and then tragic death of his first wife in a car accident shortly thereafter. Think about all the expectations he must have had for his budding family, only to have all his dreams destroyed in a matter of moments. Death is another way that love gets taken away from us and is not guaranteed.

Still through all he's endured, Keanu didn't retreat into self-isolation nor plunge into promiscuity, and he remains widely known as one of the sweetest guys you'll ever meet, loved by all. Years ago he became a viral meme for giving up his seat on the train for a woman who was carrying a large bag and again for helping a motorist on the side of the road. He's been photographed on many occasions next to female fans with his arms around them, but instead of placing his hands onto their bodies, he hovers a few inches away from them to give them some personal boundaries, a strong sign of a healthy Lover archetype.

But Keanu Reeves is not just passionately devoted to looking like a gentleman on camera. He knows John Mayer is correct that "love is a verb." Reeves had a sister who passed away of childhood cancer, so every year he quietly gives part of his earnings to leukemia research. He loves his work as well and is known for caring for and feeding cast and crew members and even giving gifts and parts of his own salary to his stunt guys. Don't forget the entire plot of John Wick revolved around the Hermit Lover who had lost his soul mate and all the people who loved him enough to help him after he stepped out of his isolation and back into the world.

Let's return to the hard truth that love is never owned nor owed, so it can never be guaranteed. In Greek mythology, this truth is taught to us through the story of Orpheus and Eurydice. Orpheus loved Eurydice so much that when she died, he followed her to the underworld using his beautiful love songs to bypass the guards and to strike a deal with Hades to take his love back to the land of the living. The only catch was: Orpheus must walk in front of Eurydice and not look back. That's right. Hades asked Orpheus to draw a boundary and turn away from his love and just trust that because she loves him, she will follow.

After a long journey out of the underworld, when they were almost free, Orpheus messed up. He allowed doubt to creep in. He began to expect the worst: that he had been tricked by Hades or Eurydice or both. He started questioning whether or not he was ever worthy enough to receive Eurydice's love or capable enough to lead her safely back home. Then he wondered if maybe he hadn't won her heart after all, as if hearts can be won, and he looked back. Eurydice was plunged back into the underworld, and Orpheus was consumed by his despair... and then quite violently dismembered and decapitated by some Dionysian church goers. As legend has it, they threw his head in the river, and it floated away still singing the same old sad love song... those Greeks really knew how to end a story. What Orpheus failed to realize was that expecting the worst is often a self-fulfilling prophesy in love.

Perhaps you've made it to this point in the chapter and have realized that you really DON'T identify with the Lover archetype or practicing loving does not seem to come naturally to you. Maybe you've struggled with romantic relationships or just feel confused about how to express love. Rather than pointing you to the traditional "love languages" idea or quoting Corinthians ("Love is patient, kind" etc.) which you've all heard before, I'd like for you to consider something that maybe you haven't heard before - that the universal currency in the economy of Love is: BEAUTY.

Plato claimed beauty leads us to the divine. Now, I know some of y'all are already shaking your ugly mugs thinking this is bad news for you, but you don't have to BE beautiful to be a great Lover, you have to learn how to **share beauty** and facilitate beautiful experiences with those you love. This is why in the tale of Orpheus, his beautiful music is his primary tool. If you know the social media creator Leo Skepi, he is a brilliant example of the Lover through his sharing of beauty. He demonstrates to his audience that home decorating, fashion, and self-care can be both stunningly beautiful AND mascu-line at the same time.

Think about courtship rituals - we give beautiful bouquets of flowers, we dress in beautiful clothes to go out and experience some-thing beautiful (an opera, a play, a meal), we watch beautiful sunsets together and whisper beautiful words in each other's ears. Why do we do this? Because beauty makes us feel a certain way! Beauty helps us bring out feelings of awe, joy, and appreciation, which are pleasant states to both be present in and remember. Interestingly, there are brain scans that show the parts of the brain that activate when people see a visual image of beauty are the same as when they hear beautiful music or watch a beautiful act of kindness take place. Think about the tale of Aladdin. He had nothing to offer Princess Jasmine except to show her the beautiful world outside the palace, and that was all she ever wanted.

How interesting is it that the patriarchy has tried to convince us that beauty and looking beautiful is inherently feminine and also that beauty standards are impossibly high (a.k.a. you can't be considered beautiful unless...)? But when we look around the natural world, it is the male in almost every species who is more brightly colored, more beautiful.

I knew a Lover once who worked in the beauty industry as a straight man. He was what could only be described as a Casanova type - absolute lady killer - although when I knew him he was in his Her-mit era, to be clear. He wasn't the most traditionally handsome man in the entire world, but he wore beautiful clothes with confidence and a little touch of mystery: lace tops, zebra striped pants, fascinat-ing jewelry. He and I talked at length about how other men objecti-fied him or teased him for appearing "feminine" but he had learned to ignore them. Think about that for a second. Men who make them-selves beautiful become targets of other men. Why is that? Could it be that in a capitalist patriarchy that rich and powerful old ugly men are threatened by dashing young gorgeous men regardless of their social status? You decide!

So what is the lesson for the modern day Lover? First, maintain necessary boundaries to not compromise your love with passion nor try to meet others' expectations. Next, release your own expectations whether they be positive (idealistic) or negative (doubtful) about love, and decide to practice loving regardless of outcomes and with grace and forgiveness for other people's choices. As Don Miguel Ruiz says: "You don't need to justify your love, you don't need to explain your love, you just need to practice your love. Practice creates the master."

Last but certainly not least, create beautiful memories with your loved ones. Sharing beauty in all its forms with the people you love is an actual practice of loving. Finding beauty outside of perfection is an actual act of grace. When the Lover releases the expectations or standards of beauty, they can extend grace to the ugly experiences in life, uncover beauty in silver linings, and forgive themselves and others to step back into the appreciation of the art of loving.

Reflection

Alright Lover-boys, before we move on to the lovers-of-laughter in Chapter 5, it's time to reflect. The Lover, with his passionate devotion, is the greatest appreciator of beauty above all things. The best Lovers have the gift to make life a little more beautiful for everyone around them. Ask questions like:

- When was the last time you shared a beautiful moment with your loved ones? How can you facilitate more beauty in your lives?
- Why do you think the concept of beauty and even the "beauty industry" is focused on women? Who benefits from convincing men that appearing beautiful or being interested in beauty is innately feminine?
- How can you release unrealistic expectations that are holding you back from loving others or yourself? How can you build

boundaries that support realistic expectations from your loved ones?

Chapter Summary

- Theme: Passion and Beauty
- Key to Growth: Forgiveness and Boundaries
- Essence: The Lover embraces passion, connection, and appreciation for beauty in all forms. A nontoxic Lover is enthusiastic, open-hearted, and forgiving.
- Pitfall to Avoid: Holding expectations, fantasizing; holding grudges, self-isolating
- Growth Focus: Cultivating emotional boundaries, practicing forgiveness, and honoring love's sacred bond with beauty.

5

The Joker

Overview

- **Description:** The Joker, or Jester, is the archetype of humor, playfulness, and truth. He challenges conventions and brings levity to life.
- **Major Conflict:** The Joker struggles with deflection and vulnerability and walks the line between frivolity and sincerity. He risks becoming either a Clown (avoiding seriousness) or a Cynic (disappointed in everyone).
- **Path to Growth:** The Joker becomes his best self by using humor to uplift and relieve the tension of others, embracing sincerity and vulnerability with courage, and finding joy in play and presence.

Stories of the Joker

> Life is a tragedy when seen in close-up, but a comedy in long-shot." – Charlie Chaplin

The patriarchy expects men to 'man up' and suppress emotions, yet some of the most emotionally aware men are those who dare to make us laugh and think. The Joker archetype reminds us that humor isn't about avoiding truth — it's about revealing it. I have a soft spot in my heart for the Joker archetype. These are the makers of dad jokes, the players of pranks, the class clowns. Jokers are who we seek out when we are feeling low. In fact, my step-father, who became a widower a decade or so ago, told me it was watching comedy movies that helped him through his grief. If you're a comedian reading this right now, remember how meaningful your work is for people you may never ever meet. To bring others joy and laughter is a precious and life-sustaining masculine gift.

Theo Von is most definitely a Joker archetype. You never know what that guy's going to say next or what mashup of truths he will suddenly improvise. The clip where Bobby Lee asks Theo to "be his dad" and he replies: "Bobbehhh," with a cajun Asian fusion accent is maybe my favorite clip of all time. If I need to laugh real quick, that's what I'm looking up, or the, "I got a Christmas Katt Williams," clip. Next time you see Theo on Joe Rogan's podcast, notice how much he makes Joe Rogan belly laugh, and it's almost always this pure-form free-association comedy that revolves around both unexpected absurdity and truth mixed together.

Even though Theo Von makes jokes for a living, he is also deeply sincere. He has meaningful friendships with other comedians, guests from his show, and fellow sobriety seekers from his Alcoholics Anonymous meetings, to whom he sends texts of encouragement and even gifts. On an episode with Mike Rowe, Mike thanks Theo for keeping in touch over time and also for modeling active listening and empathy in a way that inspires other men. Theo brings "serious" people onto his podcast and has genuine conversations with them about their work, which he has researched deeply. Even Arnold Schwarzenegger complimented Theo on doing his research before their interview. Theo punctuates with puns and absurdities to keep the levity, but not to deflect. He has repeatedly expressed sincere concern for the civilians and especially children in Gaza, even when it wasn't exactly popular to do so. He calls it like he sees it and values being honest and authentic.

My favorite type of comedy, but arguably the most angry, is SATIRE. Satire is any comedy that makes unjust powerful people or entities appear ridiculous when people are not expecting it, even though they may be thinking the same. For example, in Luke 11:42, Jesus performed some subtle satire on the Pharisees, who undoubtedly took themselves too seriously. He accused them of neglecting justice and love because they were too busy tithing (or giving ten percent of) their mint crops. This is pretty funny to anyone who has ever grown mint because you know how fast it grows!

My favorite satirist, hands down, is Bassem Youssef. Often called the "Jon Stewart of Egypt," Bassem, a heart surgeon who started doing comedy on YouTube, used satire and comedy to critique the Egyptian government and authoritarian leaders during a time of great political tension after the 2011 Arab Spring. His television show, Al-Bernameg, was the first ever live-studio-audience comedy news show in the Middle East, and became incredibly popular, blending humor with sharp social and political commentary. Through comedy, Bassem held up a mirror to Egyptian society, challenging abuses of power and censorship in ways that were accessible, clever, and disarming.

His work is a fantastic embodiment of the Joker's key strengths: using humor to reveal truth, alleviate fear, and connect with people in ways that provide them with much needed psychological relief. Despite facing threats and significant losses, he sparked critical conversations and inspired people to question authority, showing the power of humor in fostering resilience and encouraging social change even under oppressive conditions. He has since moved to the US and is continuing to speak up against injustice and occupation, reworking his entire set in English for American audiences. He has been and still is wildly successful, continuing to sell out show after show, but lately I've watched Bassem from afar confronting the Shadow side of the Joker.

So let's talk about the two toxic Shadows of the Jokers. Jokers suffer and become toxic when they either don't take things seriously enough (Clown) or take things way too seriously or personally

(Cynic). All I can hear in my mind is the Heath Ledger version of The Joker saying: "Why so serious?" We all know what a Clown is, but a Cynic is someone who has become so serious that they distrust other people's sincerity, as if everyone but themselves is self-interested or corrupted.

After October 7th, 2023, Bassem faced backlash when he appeared on the Piers Morgan show and made some very harsh jokes that reeked of cynicism masquerading as clowning. As I watched, I could tell the entire moment was too personal, too soon, too serious for him. He opened the segment by explaining how his wife's family was in Gaza and had been bombed already and that they hadn't heard from them, but it was "normal" because the Palestinian people are "hard to kill" followed by a joke about trying to kill his own wife but failing because she uses their children as "human shields."

This outraged millions because in the midst of a tragic moment that was intensely serious, he used un-seriousness or clownishness as a deflection because otherwise anything else he had to say would have been angry, blaming, or sad, which isn't exactly on-brand for a comedian. I don't use this example to pick on Bassem. He's my favorite satirist, my friend, and one of the most sincere men I've ever met. When I met him nearly a decade ago and told him about my heart condition, he listened and empathized just exactly like Mike Rowe described Theo Von doing. This is the gift of the Joker, but I bring up the example of Bassem facing his Shadow because we are all susceptible to the downward spiral, even the best of us.

Speaking of the best of us, consider Robin Williams. Robin Williams's humor, creativity, and warmth embodied the Joker's ability to bring light and levity to others. Several of his jokes became instant classics, like: "Politicians are like diapers. They need to be changed often, and for the same reason." That was a Robin Williams joke. Beyond laughter, he was known for using his humor as a form of healing and connection, encouraging others to embrace life's absurdity while staying authentic and heart centered. But that's not to say he never made an overly cynical joke. He joked once that "suicide is a permanent solution to a temporary problem" and was met with outrage. In a 2002 interview, he said: "Comedy is the art of making people laugh without making them puke. But sometimes, you cross the line, and you have to apologize."

Robin Williams was also deeply sincere. When he wasn't performing, he was visiting children in cancer wards and soldiers far away from home, sharing joy everywhere he went and helping others have a sense of play in the present moment to ease the fear of what the future may hold. It has been said that in his movies he asked that homeless people nearby the set be hired on as extras because he really understood that bringing a smile to someone's face could alter the course of their whole life.

At age 63, Robin Williams ended his own life, shocking and grieving the world. His family told of his struggles with depression and fear alongside his diagnosis of Lewy Body dementia. His untimely end showcases the darkest part of the Joker's shadow: deflection. The Joker is often keenly aware of his surroundings in order to make culturally relevant jokes. With this awareness comes strong empathy. The way the Joker confronts his Shadow is to learn how to process out strong negative emotions like fear and despair rather than avoid them. As the negative emotions accumulate, the Joker will find it harder and harder to connect and relate to others and easier and easier to want to escape reality because they are becoming disappointed, cynical, and distrusting.

Overcoming deflection is no small task. However, the best treatments are meditation and play. Meditation helps us remain in the present moment, which is essential for the charisma and comedic timing of the Joker, but they may not carry it off the stage with them. In private, many Jokers take off their "wise guy" masks and want their friends and family to take them more seriously, so they dwell on grim topics, like impending doom. If anxiety is your struggle, try a grounding meditation where you name five things you can see, four things you could touch, three things you can hear, two things you can smell, and one thing you could taste that is in your immediate environment.

This restores your mind from the future, which is where anxiety lives, and brings you back to the present, which is where you are safe.

Another antidote to cynicism and deflection is play. Think about it this way: if you are playing an extremely fun game with other people, are you actively trying to avoid the game? Are you distrusting the people in the game or thinking about the general disappointing state of the world? Of course not! You're playing! When you're having fun, you don't want to leave — ask any parent, and they'll know this unwritten rule. When you're connecting with others in a fun way (play), it soothes your cynical soul. You start to realize, folks ain't all bad, and life ain't all bad, neither.

This is actually why sports are essential to civilizations. We find evidence of games in human society as far back as 6000BC! Researcher Jane McGonigal has discussed the use of sports and public game playing in the Roman Empire. During times of social unrest, famine, or economic hardship, Roman leaders often employed a strategy known as "bread and circuses". This involved providing free food (bread) and entertainment (circuses, including games, chariot races, and gladiatorial contests) to the population to maintain morale and prevent uprisings. As it turns out, they were onto something! Play relieves stress, encourages social bonding, and builds resilience. Now McGonigal has designed her own game called SuperBetter to promote mental health and traumatic injury recovery through supportive gaming.

While it can be difficult to find joy in play when you have a heavy heart, just remember: the opposite of joy is not grief, it's disappointment. To be disappointed, you have to have expected something better than reality. If you've already learned how to release expectations, then you will find yourself less and less disappointed with outcomes and more and more grateful for the present moment. Choosing joy does not betray your grief — it helps you heal it. Cultivating joy in the midst of injustice is a form of resistance that Joker's specialize in and can help other people accomplish.

Don't use merry-making as an excuse for not processing your grief though! Toxic Jokers often use comedic deflection as a means to avoid their strong negative emotions and pain. They'll say things like: "Relax it's just a joke" or "Humor is my coping mechanism." In reality, they are hurting but think that everyone expects them to be the funny guy.

I met a Joker in college by the name of Drew Morgan. You might know him from his standup specials, appearances on Comedy Central, or his collaborations with the "Liberal Rednecks" and the WellRed tour, but if you're as lucky as I am, you know him from driving his drunk ass back to the dorms from the Cotton Eyed Joe! His wife Andi was also one of the Maryville College crew and is a force of nature in her own right — singer, song writer, actor, filmmaker, and mama extraordinaire. Remember how I said I met Bassem Youssef? Well, these two all-stars were both with me that very night. Comedy is a small world, truly.

Unfortunately, the life of a comedian is not always fun and games. Recently Drew and Andi went through a traumatic labor and delivery experience while birthing their son, full of disappointment, fear, and pain. Everyone made it through safely and are healthy and thriving now, thank God, but I remember sending Drew a really sincere message after mama and baby were in the clear telling him it was ok to not be the funny guy for a few days while he felt all the feelings of almost losing his wife. We love serious-Drew as much as we love funny-Drew, and he didn't owe anyone any levity in that moment.

Part of every Joker's lesson in life is to understand that the love and support they get from others does not depend on their own good humor. They don't have to be the entertainment to be embraced. In fact, it's the Joker's aptitude for sincerity that makes him the most magnetic in his personal and professional life. It's his sincerity, even in his most vulnerable moments, that redeems him.

If you've never really considered the meaning of the word sincere, think of it as the exact opposite of a hypocrite. A sincere person speaks and acts honestly in accordance with their truth. They don't say one thing and do another - in fact, they make fun of people who do that! In order to be sincere, you have to be authentically yourself in word and deed, marching to the beat of your own heart. Bassem was redeemed after his infamous Piers Morgan interview because he leaned into sincerity and empathy. He organized fundraisers for Palestinians. He did more and longer interviews with a wider variety of hosts and formats, including Theo Von, to speak truth to power with seriousness and sincerity and satire sprinkled in. This is the redemption of the Joker.

Dave Chappelle is an excellent example of the Joker who has made peace with his Shadow. If you don't know Dave Chappelle, do you honestly live under a rock? Just as a recap, though, Chappelle is one of the most celebrated comedians of our generation, who at the height of his success in 2005, left a $50 million contract for his comedy show on the table to move to Africa and basically disappear out of disappointment in the industry (Cynic).

Upon his return to the industry, Dave embraced vulnerability and explained that he felt overwhelmed by the pressures of fame and the direction of the show in those years. He was concerned about the impact of his comedy on society and felt that the environment had become toxic. In interviews, he famously said, "I don't want the world to change me." That's sincerity. He went on to get a contract worth ten million dollars more and for less man-hours than the one he walked away from. That's redemption.

I can't close out this chapter without bringing Josh Johnson into this conversation. Josh Johnson is a standup comedian whose success on social media got him a gig on the Daily Show with Jon Stewart (another legendary Joker). Josh is most well known for his storytelling style comedy about current events and pop culture, a highly relatable subject matter. What has always struck me about Josh's delivery is his sincerity and empathy but also his ability to paint a picture of an event for people so clearly that they get lost in the story until he smacks 'em with an unexpected punchline at the end.

My favorite example of this was the day the OceanGate submarine imploded as it was ferrying five men to see the Titanic wreckage. Obviously the subject of death is taboo, which is why we say, "Don't speak ill of the dead." But as a current events comedian, Josh knew he had to make it a part of his relief-humor set because everyone was thinking about it, but also too scared to joke about it. So he sets the crowd up by first pointing out that he feels horrible... for Logitech as a company (because of the controller used to pilot the sub). The audience laughed and loosened up. Then he pulled the crowd back to empathy by explaining that he doesn't know how to feel about the whole event, and he feels conflicted because there was a boat full of refugees that capsized on the same day and many more people died but they got no press, no public sympathy.

He then slipped in a profound truth: we have never tried to become those refugees, but we have all tried to become those billionaires, so then we are wired by our culture to pay more attention to and sympathize more with the wealthy than the poor. Finally while everyone is contemplating this statement, he lays the final punchline on them: "I just wanna know what the orcas think..." Boom! Relief laughter all around! No one in that room was expecting that line next and it cut through the mental tension of the tragic circumstances like a hot knife through butter. This is the gift of the Joker - to provide much needed psychological relief in stressful times.

Comedy is therapeutic because it helps you process out and release the fearful and painful emotions inside you. This is different than numbing your feelings entirely - which is what alcohol and opiates do. Those poisons are forms of deflection and only make the problems worse in the long run. Instead of reaching for a bottle, reach for a pen. Write a letter to your inner child and say things that you would have wanted a caring adult to say to you when you were feeling lonely, sad, angry, betrayed, or scared. Tell yourself a joke. Let your inner child laugh. You'll be surprised how effective that exercise is - no shrink required. These are ways that you acknowledge heavy feelings, understand where they are coming from (a.k.a. process them), and allow them to be released.

Remember, the Jokers play a large role as a truth teller on the stage of life, yet they often feel the loneliest, the most burdened by awareness, and the least respected. Just ask Rodney Dangerfield. But I hope what you learned from this chapter is that we love having you all around - you bring us joy when we need it most. Please continue to be true to yourselves while combatting cynicism with playfulness and presence, and fending off foolishness with sincerity. Don't be afraid to seek help when you need it. No shame in the healing game.

Reflection

"I got clowns to the left of me, jokers to the right, and here I am, stuck in the middle with you!" This chapter might have been the easiest for me to write because I know and love so many good men who are Jokers. Hopefully it will inspire you to lighten up a little or to explore sincerity in your relationships. Before we move on to The Hero, let's reflect:

- How do you use deflection to avoid painful or fearful emotions? How could you understand and process those emotions and release them instead?
- What can you do to be more playful in your life or with your loved ones?
- How can you become more sincere a.k.a. true to yourself and aligned with your feelings, even when they are difficult feelings to admit?

Chapter Summary
- Theme: Joy and Sincerity
- Key to Growth: Playfulness and Presence

- Essence: The Joker is light-hearted, humorous, and deeply empathetic. He brings levity to grave situations, sees the world through a lens of absurdity, and helps others take themselves less seriously.
- Pitfall to Avoid: Deflection or cynicism
- Growth Focus: Embracing humor without deflecting from personal truths, using sincerity, presence, and playfulness to build connection, and exercising empathy to bring joy to others

6

The Hero

Overview

- **Description:** The Hero represents courage, determination, and the desire to face his fears for the greater good. He is the archetype of the journey, the quest, and the triumph over adversity.
- **Major Conflict:** The Hero struggles with selfishness, seeking validation, and the fear of failure. In toxicity, the Hero either becomes risk-addicted (Cavalier) or risk-averse (Coward).
- **Path to Growth:** The Hero grows by releasing the desire for glory or certainty, learning from others, and using his gifts to restore hope to his community.

Stories of the Hero

"A Hero is someone who has given his or her life to something bigger than oneself." – Joseph Campbell

Maybe when you think of a Hero you envision the 'lone wolf' who needs no one and fears nothing, but true Heroism has always been balancing risk and reward and knowing when to ask for help. The Hero archetype reminds us that courage isn't the absence of fear — it's the choice to face fear for a greater purpose.

There are so many examples of Heroes. It's basically our favorite story to tell worldwide. It goes something like this: "A seemingly ordinary person receives a calling that launches him into a new world where he meets a wise mentor and faces trials, loss, and his deepest fears, then returns home with some treasure or truth to help his community." This is the character arc of so many characters from popular culture that I cannot possibly name them all, but just to prove a quick point: Luke Skywalker, Harry Potter, Luke Cage, Paul Atreides, Frodo Baggins, Peter Parker, Neo, Jon Snow, T'Challa, Link... All these characters and more teach us about the path of the Hero, including their Shadow-conflicts with fear and validation (which is seeking proof, reassurance, or affirmations from others.)

Let's illustrate the Hero's path and struggles with a real life story. The day was April 29, 1975, better known as the Fall of Saigon. The Vietnam War was coming to a chaotic close. Major Buang-Ly, a South Vietnamese Air Force pilot was desperate to escape the advancing North Vietnamese forces with his family. His wife gave him an ultimatum: either all of them leave... or none of them. So he managed to squeeze his wife and five children into a tiny Cessna O-1 Bird Dog, a light reconnaissance plane with no room for passengers besides the pilot. With no safe place left in Vietnam, they decided to make a daring escape toward the USS Midway, an American aircraft carrier stationed off the coast.

Major Buang took off from Con Son Island, navigating without any modern equipment. As he approached the USS Midway, he began circling the massive carrier, dropping notes written on paper to signal his distress. One of his notes, weighted down with a pistol, read: "Can you move the helicopters to the other side, so I can land?" He was running out of fuel.

At first, the USS Midway's crew thought the request was impossible. The Cessna wasn't equipped for carrier landings, and there was simply no space — dozens of Huey helicopters were already packed onto the flight deck. An order came down from the Admiral to have the family land in the water, where they would have surely died.

However, Captain Lawrence Chambers, the first African American commander of an aircraft carrier, made a bold decision: he ordered sailors to push helicopters overboard to clear enough room for Major Buang to land. Some of these helicopters were worth millions of dollars, but human lives took priority. With a makeshift runway now open, Major Buang expertly landed the tiny Cessna on the carrier deck, despite having no tailhook or carrier-specific modifications. His skillful landing — without even a bump — earned the cheers of the sailors watching. Major Buang and his family were welcomed aboard as Heroes. The sailors raised his children onto their shoulders and celebrated the preservation of life, after having witnessed so much death.

Captain Chambers heard the call and stepped outside of his comfort zone to answer it. If he had prioritized the validation of his superior officers and property over people, he would have let Major Buang and his family drown. Had he tried to be a savior singlehandedly, he would have never been able to clear the deck by himself. Not only did he reject validation, but he also knew when to ask for assistance. This is the hallmark of the healthy Hero.

Similarly, Major Buang himself had to reject validation of "the odds." Think about this for a moment. The odds were against Buang's family's escape: the plane was too small, safety was too far, the fuel was too little. All the statistics were stacked against him. Had he waited for the probability math to work in his favor (external validation), it would have been too late. But the Hero knows that the call comes, whether or not the odds are favorable. Then as he flew by the aircraft carrier, he was more than willing to ask for assistance. His hope was for his family's survival after all that they had endured. Major Buang was his family's Hero as much as Captain Chambers was that day, or perhaps even more. Today, Major Buang's Cessna O-1 Bird Dog is on display at the National Naval Aviation Museum in Florida as a testament to this extraordinary moment in history.

The fear of the day was met by the courage of Buang, Chambers, and every person on that deck. Because they worked together valiantly and refused to give up, they brought much needed hope to humanity in the wake of a dark and tragic war. This is the gift of the Hero.

In 1949, author Joseph Campbell published his seminal work called "The Hero with a Thousand Faces" which describes what he calls "the mono-myth" of the Hero, otherwise known as the Hero's Journey. The Hero's Journey is three parts: the Departure, the Initiation, and the Return. Each of these parts contains their own milestones.

The Departure phase includes receiving a call from the Universe in some way - maybe a job offer, maybe a cryptic letter, maybe a hologram programmed into an old droid. You'll know the call because it will be taking you away from your mundane life and leading you somewhere new and different, either physically or spiritually. The call is usually followed by the arrival of some mentor who will give you advice or tools to complete your journey. The final part of the Departure phase is crossing the threshold and stepping into the new world, where fear and uncertainty awaits you.

During the Initiation phase, the Hero goes through trials, meets allies and adversaries, and prepares himself to face the "final boss," so to speak. Joseph Campbell called the next part "The Ordeal," and it's when the Hero confronts his most frightening challenge, usually risking his life in the process. The Hero possibly falls into the "Dark Night of the Soul" where he experiences great wounding or loss of his mentor or other allies and feels utterly alone, relying solely on his own strength to continue forward to face his greatest fear: failure. Finally, the Hero overcomes the challenge and takes the treasure.

The Return phase can be the toughest for the Hero. They often face one final test of their own personal transformation right before they make it home, just to make sure their heart is in the right place to use their treasure wisely. The Hero who survives always arrives home forever changed by his adventure, ready to restore some hope and vitality to his home world.

Some would say the story of Christ is the ultimate Hero's journey. His Departure phase begins when his cousin John baptizes Jesus in the Jordan River. He leaves his home in Nazareth and meets his allies, Peter, John, and the rest, and his adversaries, the Pharisees. He faces trials and temptations right up until he underwent his own Dark Night of the Soul in the Garden of Gethsemane where he was betrayed. Then he walked bravely into his Ordeal: crucifixion. On his return, he was met with doubters, like Thomas, and friends who didn't recognize him, because ultimately the final test for Jesus as a Hero was a test of others' faith or belief in him. Finally, he brought back a hope-giving treasure to share with his community: the map to eternal life.

For an example that is a couple thousand years closer to present, let's go back to the night of August 2, 1943 and put ourselves in the Pacific Ocean on a small but quick American Naval patrol boat tasked with disrupting Japanese supply lines in the Solomon Islands. The commander of the mission is a 26 year old handsome guy by the name of John Fitzgerald Kennedy, you may have heard of him. The night of August 2nd, Kennedy's craft was struck by a Japanese destroyer which cut the American boat in half, killing two men and leaving the other eleven men in hostile waters. After Kennedy gathered the surviving crew and fashioned a makeshift raft to keep them afloat and together, he swam to the nearest island, towing his injured and severely burned shipmate, Patrick McMahon, by gripping McMahon's life jacket strap with his teeth and swimming for hours through the dark and dangerous sea until they reached the shore.

But even though they survived the Ordeal, they still faced an insane Return journey. Over the next several days, Kennedy and his crew moved around and between islands, avoiding Japanese patrols and surviving on coconuts and rainwater. On August 8th, the team was rescued by the US Navy who had received the S.O.S. that Kennedy had carved into a coconut shell and gave to two Ally-friendly Solomon Islanders who passed the message along to an Australian coast-watcher who then got it to the Americans. John F. Kennedy was awarded the Purple Heart and the Navy and Marine Corps medal for "extremely heroic conduct."

Later in his life as President of the United States, Kennedy again demonstrated qualities of courage, resilience, and innovative thinking, which are central to the Hero's journey. Kennedy's stance during the Cuban Missile Crisis, for example, reflected the Hero's willingness to face immense challenges with unflinching diplomacy, holding steadfast to the ultimate goal of protecting others. By establishing a direct line of communication between Washington and Moscow, Kennedy sought to lead not through fear, but through a bravery inspired by a higher calling. His dedication to ambitious goals like the space race embodied the Hero's drive to take risks and inspire others. His famous challenge to "ask not what your country can do for you — ask what you can do for your country" captures the Hero's call to selfless service and the pursuit of the greater good for his community. JFK's leadership was marked by his optimism and idealism, qualities that encouraged people to envision a better future and unite toward common goals. While his journey was tragically cut short, his life and legacy continue to live on, fitting the archetype of the Hero as someone who faces trials with valor, lifting others through perseverance and hope.

Now that you're getting the picture of the nontoxic Hero, let's discuss how Heroes can become toxic. At the center of the Hero's journey is the Hero's relationship to fear and risk-taking. Every Hero is called to step out of their comfort zone and take risks in order to gain some value that they can bring back to their family or community. The first way the Hero becomes toxic is if they become obsessed with taking vain risks for the adrenaline rush or the attention and not because those risks will benefit others. Just like the hedonistic Lover becomes "addicted" to love and sensuality, the Cavalier Hero becomes "addicted" to risky behavior, physically, financially or both.

This stems from the internal drive of the Hero to face his fears combined with the need for external validation in the form of attention, praise, or glory. The toxic Cavalier Hero thinks his value depends on his fearlessness and victories, that the "treasure" he provides is in inspiring others to take risks. However, the Cavalier has often lost the plot. They become Homelander instead of Superman without heeding "the call" to a higher purpose of serving others and restoring hope to the hopeless. The main question a Cavalier Hero must ask himself in order to grow is: Am I listening for the call? Most Cavalier Heroes are too busy galavanting around seeking adrenaline that they are not listening when someone calls out for a Hero. Channeling your heroic actions through mindful awareness of others and their needs is the path forward.

On the opposite side of this coin, the Coward Hero shivers in his boots. The toxic Coward Hero is risk-averse, or reluctant to take risks. He avoids facing his fears or putting himself in danger of any kind. At the root of cowardly behavior is usually someone who has experienced violent childhood trauma and/or traumatic failures — the kinds of failures that are humiliating or public and stick in your mind long after they've been forgotten by others. The Coward is stuck in a place of fearfulness and thus does not heed "the call" in his own life either, not because he can't hear it, but because he's ignoring it. This, too, is selfish. Joseph Campbell said, "When we quit thinking primarily about ourselves and our own self-preservation, we undergo a truly heroic transformation of consciousness."

The most important step any Hero can take toward healing is seeking a mentor. The mentor in the Hero's journey is always the person who provides the Hero with the tools and encouragement he needs to shoot for the stars while still keeping his feet on the ground. The mentor often has more faith in the Hero than the Hero has in himself, but he might show him "tough love." The mentor teaches the Hero that failure is inevitable, but giving up is optional. Think about the role of Albus Dumbledore to Harry Potter or Obi Wan Kenobi to Luke Skywalker. The mentor also reminds the Hero of the higher purpose of his mission: the greater good. Most Heroes don't ever retire — they just become mentors, and this is a vital role to continue for men and boys.

The story of the Hero resonates with people because so many of us on some level are all called out of our comfort zones to face our fears and return with treasure and hope. On Theo Von's podcast, Richard Reeves, the President of the American Institute of Boys and Men, recounted how when his father was unemployed at one time, he still got up each morning and dressed himself as if for work. When Richard asked his father why he did this when he didn't have a job, his father replied that he did have a job — and that was finding a new job to provide for his family. These types of encounters show what's called "the Every Man" Hero, who is an ordinary man with extraordinary tenacity and courage in the face of adversity. The man who knows how to listen for the call and look for the needs in his community that he can step up to fill even when he might fail, with the purpose of providing value to his family and neighbors — that is the Hero, just as much as the knight-in-shining-armor slaying the dragon to save the Princess is. It may not be as glamorous or as celebrated, but it's essentially the same story.

When the Hero submits to both the call of need in their community and the guidance of a mentor, he cultivates something called "interdependence." In the next chapter, we will be talking about interdependence in the context of the Caregiver, who struggles with codependence , but the Hero is almost the opposite of the Caregiver in that he struggles with independence - trying to take on everything by himself. Have you ever heard the phrase, "Don't be a Hero!"? That means: don't try to do everything, all at once, by yourself. This is a lesson for the Hero archetype. Adopting a mentor means that you are the kind of Hero who knows how to ask for help and not be independent to a fault.

Don't confuse asking for assistance with seeking validation, nor heroism with saviorism. If the Hero leans too far into interdependence, he can end up in codependence just like anyone can. This happens in one of two ways: the Coward Hero can become too dependent on his mentor (private validation), and the Cavalier Hero can become too obsessed with proving how much of a Hero he is (public validation). Incidentally, have you noticed how many Hero stories include masking the Hero's identity? This is to guard the Cavalier Hero from too much glory (public validation), which can corrupt his ego as well as cloud his judgment. Likewise, have you noticed how many Hero stories include the death of the mentor? This is to push the Coward Hero into facing his Ordeal without private validation. The number one place we all seek validation is from our parents. Is it a coincidence that so many Hero stories are about orphans? You decide!

When the Hero matures into healthy interdependence and transcends the need for internal or external validation, he often settles into the role of the unsung Hero, taking risks to reap rewards with ease and modesty. The most heroic act I've ever witnessed in my life was committed by a group of unsung Heroes. It was the evening of my junior prom. When you're from a small town like Kingston, TN, there aren't too many venues to host large events, so we all had to ride or carpool to Knoxville that night. As I was driving west on Interstate-40 to meet my date and friends for photos, I saw a large object falling from the overpass into the eastbound lane, where it smashed into the hood of a small black car headed toward Knoxville with four of my fellow prom-goers inside. The car spun and flipped into the median and promptly caught fire.

I shifted into the emergency lane without hesitation, slammed on my breaks, and jumped out of the car — as did the students in front of me and others on the opposite side of the interstate. Six teenage boys in tuxedos ran toward the burning vehicle and freed all four of their classmates quicker than I could open my flip phone and call 9-1-1. When I reached the girls to help them climb the grassy median in their ballgowns and high heels, their little car exploded, sending a huge cloud of black smoke up, almost like it was special effects on a movie set. We all erupted into tears of relief. There's a reason people say events like this "restore their hope in humanity." Those boys didn't get any kind of medal or recognition that day, but they beautifully exemplified the role of the nontoxic Hero: to swiftly, selflessly, and courageously aid those in danger to deliver assistance and hope in time of need.

The nontoxic Hero depends on his community to let him know what their needs are so that he can take calculated risks and face risks with courage for the common good and not just for the thrill or the glory of it. Healing of the Hero requires him to be both strong and vulnerable, both self-reliant and humble enough to ask for assistance.

Reflection

"Everything that is done in the world is done by hope," the theologian Martin Luther once said. Reflect on the small ways you've acted valiantly and restored someone's hope. Maybe you volunteered to sit with someone during their chemotherapy appointments, or maybe you helped someone change a tire in the rain. Small acts of heroism help you flex that muscle for when a bigger call comes along. Consider these questions:

- How can you give someone just a little more hope for the future today even if it means facing your fears?
- Who can you mentor and help them face their fears and challenges?
- When was the last time you really engaged with calls for help within your community? How can you step out of your comfort zone and put yourself in a place to hear the cries of the hopeless near you?

Chapter Summary

- Theme: Risk and Reward
- Key to Growth: Courage and interdependence
- Essence: The Hero is known for facing danger, taking risks, and being a symbol of hope. This archetype embodies the journey of overcoming fears and learning when to ask for help.
- Pitfall to Avoid: Recklessness, vainglory; cowardice, seeking validation
- Growth Focus: Building resilience through small not-so-glorious challenges or defeats, learning from mentors, and staying grounded despite triumphs or failures.

$$7$$

The Caregiver

Overview

- **Description:** The Caregiver is the archetype of compassion, nurturing, and generosity. He is the preserver and provider for others.
- **Major Conflict:** The Caregiver struggles with the balance between giving and withholding. He risks becoming either a resentful Martyr or a codependent Enabler.
- **Path to Growth:** The Caregiver becomes his best self by avoiding overindulgence, differentiating wants from needs, and caring for others according to their needs.

Stories of the Caregiver

"Too often we underestimate the power of a touch, a smile, a kind word, a listening ear, an honest compliment, or the smallest act of caring, all of which have the potential to turn a life around." – Leo Buscaglia

We live in a world that mocks men for being 'too soft' or 'too sensitive,' yet some of the strongest men in history were also the most nurturing. The Caregiver archetype reminds us that true masculine strength isn't found in emotional distance but in the courage to care deeply. At the essence of the nontoxic Caregiver is the ability to provide a safe space for big breakdowns and even bigger breakthroughs and preserve life through generosity and care.

The purest example of the Caregiver archetype that I can think of is Fred Rogers from "Mister Rogers' Neighborhood," the popular children's show. Mister Rogers was often criticized for his gentleness, but he didn't let that stop him from being a calm and guiding fatherly presence for countless children in America. To be clear, though, Fred Rogers wasn't just a gentleman or a "nice" guy — he trained in child development, psychology, and theology. He believed his work was a "ministry of care." He tackled tough topics like disability, racism, divorce, war, and death — even tragedies like the Challenger explosion — explaining them with great care so that children could process these situations even though they had no control over them. He encouraged his viewers to observe their negative emotions like anger, jealousy, sadness, and fear without shame. He often said, "I love you just the way you are." This is the gift of the nontoxic Caregiver.

But unfortunately, this archetype is probably the most emasculated by capitalist patriarchy of all. There's an old dad joke that says: my dad told me to get him something for Father's Day that the whole family could enjoy... so I got him a wallet! While I admit this joke is funny, it's also not that funny. Somewhere right around the Industrial Revolution, we demoted the masculine archetype of Caregiver into the role of "bread winner." This change, although it may seem like a small difference of vocabulary, has been absolutely devastating to families. A "bread winner" provides money and material things. A Caregiver provides so much more than that!

The Caregiver archetype is essentially the world's greatest Dad. Not only does he provide food and shelter, but he also provides protection and playfulness. He provides the best bear hugs, the most epic barbecues, and the sweetest prayers. He provides necessary boundaries and also opportunities to test your freedom and limits. He provides joyful assistance to the women, children, and other men in his life whenever there is a problem to solve or a pain to soothe. When we confuse "provider" for "money-maker" we have lost an enormous part of the meaning and purpose of the Caregiver.

But before the coining of the term "bread winner" - the masculine role of Caregiver was already being subverted. There is a particularly insidious lie in our popular culture that goes like this: for thousands of years, men were strictly hunters, who left their families for long stretches of time with their little 'band of brothers' to war against neighboring men and track down wild game to provide for their families who would feast upon their return, while the women were gatherers, handling all domestic tasks like child-rearing, organizing, and cooking, mostly by themselves. Do you know this story? Who told it to you? If you can't remember, it's because that's the colonizers' story. Any colonizer wants to maximize man-power for their own gain. How convenient that they tell us this story, then send our men to work in the mines and fight in the wars, where they are expected not to feel guilty about leaving their families for 8-24 hours a day 5-7 days a week because that's what real men did back in the old days, right? Right? This is emasculation of the Caregiver in service to the capitalist patriarchy.

Ask a Native American, and they'll tell you the gendered division of caregiving is NOT natural order, and NOT how families operated for eons. If you think about mothers and fathers in an indigenous, tribal setting, once children reached toddler age, their fathers would have become their majority caretakers, as the mothers would have been engaged with infant care and nursing of their siblings as well as being the primary agriculturalists because women have a greater eye for detail and color variation. Most First Nations gave women roles of leadership and let them join the hunts and even become warriors. In Pueblo cultures, women served as the primary architects and home-builders. Who do you think was protecting their children while they piled up the adobe? Their fathers! Their uncles! The idea that men should work while women stayed home was introduced to North America by the Puritans, not engrained in our shared ancient past.

And the degradation of fatherhood didn't stop with the Victorian Age. Consider how many fathers were violently separated from their children during slavery, during Jim Crow, during war after war after war. Post-1960s, as rates of divorce, children being born to single mothers, and male incarceration all rose, the societal valuing of fatherhood further declined. "Anything you can do, I can do better" became a feminist slogan, and throughout the 80s and 90s in much of popular media, the father figure was reduced to either an absent bread winner or a careless clown who can just barely manage his household without his wife. At first it was goofy-but-lovable portrayals of dads, like Homer Simpson or Carl Winslow, but later it became slapstick-buffoonery type characters, like Tim "The Toolman" Taylor, Ray Barone, and Dan Conner. Remember Daddy Daycare? At the max of this trend of clowning dads is Peter Griffin of Family Guy. I enjoy "dad jokes," but I cannot stand how they've made dads into a joke.

This over-representation of fathers as childish, immature, inept, or chronically irresponsible has eroded our collective remembering and honoring of men as divine Caregivers. It also perpetuates one of the patriarchy's favorite tropes which is: as a good man, I should just stay out of the women's way and let them manage all household and caregiving responsibilities because they are clearly more talented in domestic coordination, and I would probably just mess things up. This is emasculation of the Caregiver!! This perversion of our understanding of men's roles has led us to having whole industries of care like nursing, childcare, and education be female-dominated and largely considered "women's work" when that is just not the case!

I'm not sure who these trends benefit (though I suspect colonizers), but I'm certain it's not families. Research shows that children with involved, caring fathers (biological or not, rich or poor, married or not) are more likely to:

- Do well academically,
- Have higher self-esteem,
- Show fewer behavioral problems,

- Avoid risky behavior during adolescence, and
- Thrive in long-term relationships.

Why? Because father figures have certain masculine caregiving qualities that complement the mother's feminine ones. For example, the mother's instinct is always to safeguard her young - like a mother hen or a mama bear. Mothers spend quite a lot of time telling children "get down from there" or "stop that" while fathers are more likely to let children explore and push their own limits. It isn't that fathers are careless - they spring into action with catlike reflexes if their child is truly in danger. They are just far more risk-tolerant, like we talked about in the Hero chapter.

The masculine tendency to say "dust yourself off and try again, kid" is great for children's self esteem and autonomy. The "helicopter dad" model arose as a way for dads to "prove" they care by adopting the feminine traits of worrying and nagging, when in reality, that's a perversion of the masculine Caregiver. The masculine Caregiver is more like a coach who is training the future generation to survive on their own. Additionally, masculine Caregivers are more likely than feminine Caregivers to encourage rowdy, physical play - what my own mother used to call "rough-housing." This kind of play teaches children about boundaries, conflict resolution, and tenacity. This is not to say that all masculine Caregivers are perpetually rowdy — for one of the main gifts of the nontoxic Caregiver is to provide emotional and physical safety and security, just like with Mister Rogers.

When my brother Blake was a child, he was especially rowdy and liked to test out his "Ninja Turtle moves" on me, his unwilling and often unsuspecting sparring partner. Instead of indulging this behavior and letting my brother do whatever he wanted (because "boys will be boys"), my dad decided to give him what he needed: discipline. Dad signed himself and Blake up for Tae Kwon Do with a small Korean Caregiver named Master Eun. Now, my dad is a big guy, but Master Eun, who was a full foot shorter than him, could swiftly and easily flip him onto the mat. Maybe this doesn't sound particularly caring or nurturing by the popular (feminine) definition, but within every session at the dojo, Master Eun instilled the importance of respect, safety, self-control, and caring for all life, including one's own.

In one of his lessons about self defense, Master Eun approached my dad in front of a class full of younger pupils with a prop gun in hand, and shouted in his thick Korean accent, "MISTER CHASTEEN! What do you do if I pull a gun on you and say, 'I'm going to take your money'?!"

Dad replied, "I'd tell you no, you can't have my money, Sensei!"

"WRONG!" Eun exclaimed. "You pull out your wallet and give me your money because your life is always worth more than your money!!"

Dad laughed at the truth in this principle, then Master Eun shouted again, "MISTER CHASTEEN!! What do you do if I pull a gun on you and say, 'I'm going to take your life'?!"

"I'd tell you no, you can't have my life," he answered, shaking his head for emphasis.

"CORRECT!" Eun slapped the prop gun into my father's hand and motioned for him to hold it up like the aggressor. "You say: NOT TO-DAY!" Then he taught the class how to snatch a pistol right out of someone's hand and turn it around on them faster than they could blink. He ended the lesson by explaining that there is only honor in fighting when it is to protect and defend life — not money, not property, not reputation. Through his training, Master Eun increased his students' sense of security and autonomy while at the same time reinforcing a culture of honor, responsibility, and great carefulness. This is the divine role of the masculine Caregiver. Is it any wonder that my brother now takes his own boys to lessons with Master Eun, who is still kicking (literally) in 2025?

Speaking of great teachers from the East, Jesus of Nazareth portrays a slightly more nurturing example of the nontoxic Caregiver in the story of him feeding the five thousand. In Matthew 14 and John 6, the gospels recount the story of Jesus on the shore of the Sea of Galilee where he had been healing the sick and a large crowd had gathered.

Matthew points out that the reason Jesus was even by the sea was to mourn his cousin John the Baptist, but because he had "great compassion" for the crowd that followed him, he began healing them.

As evening approached, the disciples urged Jesus to send the crowd away so that they could find food, but instead, Jesus said, "Tell the women to make them sandwiches!" Just kidding! He took the 5 loaves and 2 fishes that a young boy offered him, prayed over it, and divided it to feed all 5,000 people. This classic miracle teaches us a very important lesson about Caregiver-Jesus: he is not a bread winner; he is a bread multiplier. He could make a little go a long way through sincere faith, compassion, and care about the people near him and their wellbeing. The nontoxic Caregiver understands that the more you give to those in need, the more you will have to give.

This brings us to a way Caregivers can become toxic: being overly generous to people who are not actually in need. This type of vain-generosity has created the "bank of dad" trope, in which dads indulge their spoiled children and can "never say no" to opening their wallets especially for their daughters. This idea serves capitalism just fine but creates resentment between men and their families because men feel as if they are required to constantly give all they have and in some cases receive very little in return. It positions men as both bread-winner and bread-loser.

Consider the story of Death of a Salesman, where the main character Willy Loman spent his life trying to obtain financial security for his family, and in the end, crashes his own car thinking his life insurance policy would be worth more to his loved ones than his presence. Willy ruined his relationships with his children and neglected his wife in pursuit of bread winning, instead of fulfilling the role of divine Caregiver. He longs for love and respect from his family, yet he doesn't realize that the connection he desires would have very easily been achieved by taking the time to actually learn about their needs, rather than assuming all they needed was money.

The lack of understanding around need-based-care has made a pushover and doormat of many a Caregiver. When men become "people pleasers" it is usually some version of this misunderstanding. It is easy for someone who carries the Caregiver archetype to give generously — it's in their nature! So when some kind of tragic or traumatic loss occurs early in these men's lives, it can result in over-compensation through giving as a way to maintain connections and relationships. Sometimes this looks like over-giving to friends or to one's career and neglecting the family, who will inherit the father's "legacy" and "work ethic" when the father is gone like with Willy Loman, but sometimes it looks like over-giving to one's family or certain members of one's family and not others.

King Lear provides a fascinating example of the toxic Caregiver. He decides to divide his kingdom among his three daughters based on how well they express their love for him (people pleaser alert!). Rather than giving according to each daughter's need, Lear gives according to "who wants it most," causing his least greedy daughter to become lost to him. He gave according to his ego and suffered for it. This is a blend of the toxic King who shows favoritism, and the toxic Caregiver who gives to please himself.

So if on one hand, the toxic Caregiver can show up as the Willy Loman type, the well-meaning but misguided Martyr who sacrifices his relationships on the altar of bread winning, then what is on the other hand? The other side of the toxic Caregiver is the Enabler, the indulger. Think of Veruca Salt's father in Willy Wonka, as Veruca screams, "I want the Golden Goose, and I want it now!!" and Mr. Salt demands, "Name your price!" despite Wonka saying the goose is not for sale.

This toxic Caregiver is quick to enable addiction, entitlement, or abuse in their loved ones because they believe any withdrawal of resources is abandoning their role as "Bank of Dad" — so they continue to indulge, to satisfy the bottomless desires of others even if the generosity is not actually in the other person's best interest. This, too, is a form of codependency, just on the enabling side of the codependent coin. The Enabler Caregiver can become themselves addicted to this vain-generosity because they secretly like feeling needed.

So how do you become a Caregiver instead of an Enabler? The way to heal this is to better understand the difference between needs and desires. Dr. Marshall Rosenberg has done phenomenal work on "nonviolent communication" - which I think could be called "caring communication." His formula for having productive conversations surrounding conflict is simple - fill in the parentheses in the following sentences: "When I observe (behavior/speech of the other person) then I feel (emotion) because I need (human need). Would you be willing to do (different behavior that helps meet the human need) instead?" Obviously the more well-versed you are in emotion-words and human needs, the easier this strategy becomes. There are nine categories of universal human needs:

- Survival & Sustenance
- Safety & Peace
- Connection & Love
- Understanding & Empathy
- Honesty & Integrity
- Recreation & Celebration
- Belonging & Interdependence
- Autonomy & Independence
- Meaning & Creativity

When the Caregiver learns to distinguish these true human needs from simple passions or desires, they and their loved ones all benefit. For example, how can children who have been spoiled by an overindulgent Caregiver fully develop their own autonomy and independence? They can't! That's why the enabler-Caregiver is part of the codependent equation. If you think this chapter describes you, I encourage you to search the full list of human needs and print it out. Then when you are tempted to give to someone, ask yourself: Will this truly meet a need for this person?

Let's use an example to illustrate this practice. Do you remember the Andy Griffith Show? In one episode, Opie, Andy Taylor's son, kills a mother bird with his slingshot (or "flip" if you're from the southern Appalachias). In that moment, what Opie desires most is to avoid taking responsibility and forget the whole thing. Instead of indulging him, Andy insists that Opie be honest and feed the baby birds as penance and accountability for his lack of care.

Andy Griffith Show has a surprising number of these examples, though I suppose it isn't all that surprising considering Andy Taylor is certainly representative of the masculine Caregiver. He doesn't just care for Opie - he cares for everyone in Mayberry, according to their needs. He knows when to give and when to withhold generosity, such as with Otis, the town drunk, whom Andy treats with firmness and fairness, but without judgment or superiority. Honestly, Andy Taylor is one of the most nontoxic father figures in modern media. He's certainly a contrast to Peter Griffin, no?

The final lesson for the Caregiver is to avoid burnout. Often the Caregiver type over-gives, over-extends, over-commits, and then is hard on himself if he doesn't meet the mark. Listen carefully, fellas: you do not have to be all things for all people in order to be effective as a Caregiver. Consider the Good Samaritan story told by Jesus. The Good Samaritan was someone who found a foreign man on the side of the road, beaten by robbers and left for dead. The Samaritan rescued the man, clothed him, and paid for his stay in a nearby inn until he recovered. Imagine if the Samaritan had refused to help because it might have taken away from his own children's inheritance. Alternatively, imagine if the Samaritan had neglected his own family to give everything he had to the stranger. This parable shows how important it is for the Caregiver to strike a balance between giving and enabling.

One more note on care before we move on to the Sage: consider the modern cliche "real men don't cry" and ask yourself, "If that's true, then why did Jesus weep?" Crying is a sign of deep care. If there's one thing I can tell you about the Chasteens (my father's family) is that we are criers. In fact, it's almost contagious. We joke about having to close our eyes while we sing moving hymns because if one of us starts crying, it's over for the rest of us! My dad says tears are pure love that pours from your eyes because Jesus squeezed your heart. They are indeed sacred offerings of care and the mark of a divine Caregiver.

If you learned nothing else from this chapter, I hope you can at least be proud going forward of how deeply you care and know that your softness or ability to yield is not a sign of weakness but of a mighty life-preserver who is able to keep others afloat. To all the great dads, coaches, teachers, nurses, and doctors out there: we appreciate and value the care you provide.

Reflection

Care like a man! Is it time to tap into your nontoxic masculine Caregiver energy? Here are some questions to ponder as you do:

- Which of the human needs are not being met in your own life and relationships? How can you facilitate those needs getting met for yourself and others?
- Does it always cost money to meet others' needs? Review the list of need categories and find one that you can provide today for someone in your life for low or no cost. How did providing in a non-monetary way make you feel?
- How can you balance "bread winning" and career exploits with nurturing family and other relationships? What is stopping you from finding this balance?

Chapter Summary
- Theme: Compassion and Generosity
- Key to Growth: Conscientiousness and Connection
- Essence: The Caregiver is nurturing, protective, and deeply generous. This archetype represents the power of caring and the strength found in providing help for others.
- Pitfall to Avoid: Enabling or indulging to please and gratify rather than to provide for others' needs.

- Growth Focus: Understanding the difference between need and desire and how to give with the most impact

8

The Sage

Overview

- **Description:** The Sage represents wisdom and truth. He is the seeker of understanding and the guide who illuminates the path for others.
- **Major Conflict:** The Sage struggles with the tension between knowledge and wonder. He risks becoming either set in his ways (Dogmatic) or paralyzed by overthinking (Cryptic).
- **Path to Growth:** The Sage grows by seeking clarity, disciplining the ego, and staying curious about the truth.

Stories of the Sage

"The only true wisdom is in knowing you know nothing." – Socrates

Have you noticed how lately intelligence is often weaponized to put people down instead of shared to lift people up? The Sage archetype reminds us that true wisdom is meant to light the path for others. From Merlin to Gandalf the Grey, Albus Dumbledore to Yoda - representations of the Sage are all around us. However, this character is almost always cast as a side-kick or mentor, so very rarely do we experience the entire story arc of the Sage.

Think about it. When we meet Yoda in Star Wars, he's already multiple centuries old. All we really know about Yoda's journey is that he became a wise old teacher who speaks in riddles and doesn't understand grammar. Similarly, Albus Dumbledore is already elderly when Harry Potter and friends meet him, and his interactions with them along the way are cryptic and mysterious. This similarity gives us a hint to the nature of the Sage's key struggle: transforming confusion into clarity through wisdom and wonder.

One of my favorite Sages of modern history was Thich Nhat Hanh. Born in 1926, he became a monk in the Vietnamese Zen tradition at age 16 and went on to become a Zen master, peace activist, poet and global spiritual guru. He's widely considered the father of modern mindfulness practices and worked tirelessly for nonviolent solutions during the Vietnam War, which led to him being exiled from Vietnam for nearly 40 years. In 1966 he met Martin Luther King Jr., who nominated Hanh for a Nobel Peace Prize. In his lifetime, Thich Nhat Hanh wrote over 100 books on spiritual wisdom and hosted many mindfulness retreats for veterans and victims of war. His work is the embodiment of clarity without ego.

My high school calculus teacher, Mr. Bryan Friddle, was a prime example of the nontoxic Sage at work in my own life. Mr. Friddle was born of the "hippie" era and wore a prominent mustache that reminded me of Cheech Marin. He was an excellent teacher, but after the first six weeks of his class, my grade was a D-, even though I had been a straight-A+ student up until this point and was in the running for Valedictorian. Mr. Friddle could have arrogantly dismissed me as "not trying hard enough" and let me ruin my grade point average. But instead, he was determined to help me transform my confusion into clarity so that I could pull up my grade.

He started tutoring me one-on-one during his lunch break every day. He realized that even though I had passed previous math classes with good grades, I wasn't connecting the dots all the way through.

He took me back to the very basics of algebra and tied together all the concepts from the foundational level up to calculus. I can remember the exact day that it "clicked," and I finally understood. I brought my grade up to an A and passed the Advanced Placement Calculus test with the highest score possible. Mr. Friddle was so proud, and I was so grateful that he had approached me from a place of wisdom instead of a place of ego.

The first way that the Sage becomes toxic is through letting his ego run the show. The Dogmatist is the Sage who becomes so full of knowledge that he stops seeking truth that might disrupt his beliefs and prefers lies that reinforce his worldview. Read that sentence again. To say it another way, the toxic Sage lets his head overrule his heart, sometimes resulting in heartless beliefs and behaviors that are propped up by lies and arrogance.

Consider Walter White from the television show Breaking Bad. At first, Walt is a high school chemistry teacher with a pregnant wife and a teenage son who has cerebral palsy. When he receives a terminal lung cancer diagnosis, knowing his salary is modest and his savings meager, he begins his spiral into the toxic Sage and diverts from a path of truth and wisdom onto a path of deception and arrogance. The primary lie he tells himself over and over is that he's manufacturing and selling meth on behalf of his family, for their future safety and financial security after he is dead. But in the end (spoiler alert), after he faced his own shadow, Walt admits the truth. He tells his wife that it was all for him. "I did it for me. I liked it. I was good at it. And I was really… I was alive." Telling this truth was an important part of his redemption.

Walter White's example teaches us a powerful lesson about the Dogmatic Sage: they care more about being "right" than being "truthful". Walt genuinely thought he had a good and morally justifiable (right) plan while completely ignoring or rejecting any evidence (truth) contrary to his plan. He became the "mad scientist" through this process of stacking one lie on top of another on top of another to justify using his wisdom for purely personal gain and prowess. Every time he chose a lie over the truth, he became more invested in his dark and selfish obsessions. He convinced himself that the ends would justify the means if he could just reach the next milestone, make one more deal. Maybe that was the most insidious lie of all - that he would be able to simply walk away whenever he wanted and escape the cycle as well as the inevitable consequences.

There are a lot of what people would label "narcissists" and "cult leaders" in the toxic Dogmatic Sage category. Tom Riddle who later became Lord Voldemort in the Harry Potter series is a fantastic example of a narcissistic boy who was practically a genius yet chose to reject truth and curiosity, opting instead for dogma based in vicious, divisive lies like "powerful people (wizards) should be allowed to persecute and murder less powerful people (muggles)." You can especially see the crossover from the Magician archetype in Voldemort as he becomes ever-more obsessed with power but also immortality, which is very much in the Sage realm. The toxic Sage is always trying to "outsmart" their opponents, whether they be physical human opponents or supernatural opponents like fate, death, or even God. Think about how deeply narcissistic this is. This is why so many are obsessed with immortality.

Maybe you think the Philosopher's Stone was just invented for the Harry Potter series, but according to Von Helmont's History of the Tartars, a young man known as Paracelsus went to Constantinople in 1521 and was allegedly given a Philosopher's Stone - which could perform two important tasks: transmute metals (such as from lead to gold) and provide the "elixir of life" which granted immortality and/or eternal youth. Occultists and secret societies like Freemasons have known about these stories for centuries. So not only are toxic Sages trying to outsmart death, they're also lying, confusing the history, and excluding the masses, hiding their wisdom from those they deem "unworthy" - very much like Voldemort. Consider how the ruling elite and the Roman Catholic Church treated Galileo for breaking from their dogma and claiming the Earth rotates around the sun and not vice versa. Dogmatic Sages hiding knowledge to uphold their own authority is one of the oldest stories in the book!

Another example of the toxic Sage is Anakin Skywalker from Star Wars. If you recall, Anakin as a child was highly intuitive and gifted in the Force. He had visions and dreams of the future, a highly sought after skill in the Jedi (Sage) and Sith (Magician) communities. Notably he dreamed of his own mother's death shortly before it occurred, a traumatic event that sets the stage for his downfall. But upon envisioning his lover Padme's death, Anakin starts to spiral in to the dark shadow of the Sage. He begins with lying to himself that he can "save Padme" and outsmart fate. He becomes arrogant and self-centered, rejecting the teachings of the Jedi Order in his attempts to change the future. He believes Palpatine's deceptions as well, like "Good is a point of view." Can you see how this is a perversion of truth?

Eventually Anakin's prophecy becomes a self-fulfilling one. He not only loses the love of his life, but he also loses himself in the process. He became so entangled in the deceptions of the Dark Side that he transformed into Darth Vader. Notice, too, how at the end of his story, redemption begins when he admits the truth to Luke, "I am your father," and is completed when he accepts the truth back from Luke, "I am a Jedi like my father before me," which essentially freed Anakin from the lie he had been carrying that he was destined to be a Sith, that there was no turning back, no forgiveness, no mercy. He destroys Palpatine and saves Luke, then in his final scene, allows his life support, which was essentially giving him a level of immortality, to be removed so that he can look upon his son with his own eyes before joining Padme and the Jedi Masters in the afterlife.

Truth-telling is the gift of the Sage, but confusion and toxicity seeps in when truth is conflated with knowledge. Knowledge resides in the head; truth resides in the heart. Remember Jeremiah 29:13 says, "You will seek me (God) and find me when you seek me with all your heart." Proverbs 3:5 similarly commands, "Trust in the Lord with all your heart and lean not on your own understanding (knowledge)." Isaiah 29:13 further drives home the same point, "These people come near to me with their mouth and honor me with their lips, but their hearts are far from me. Their worship of me is based merely on human rules they have been taught (knowledge, dogma)." This teaches us something powerful about the Sage: they MUST get out of their own heads - and in some cases get their heads out of their own asses.

The secondary version of the toxic Sage is the "absent-minded professor." This type of Sage, which we can call the Cryptic Sage, is constantly over-thinking, lost in his own thoughts, often suffering from analysis-paralysis. When he tries to deliver an important truth, his message is almost always misunderstood or completely indecipherable by his intended audience. Think about the 1960s cartoon film The Sword in the Stone where the Sage Merlin is attempting to train the young squire, soon-to-be-king, Arthur. Arthur spends more than half the movie in a state of perpetual confusion trying to make sense of Merlin's ramblings about the future and unorthodox life lessons that seemingly have no point other than to place Arthur in peril. The Cryptic Sage is obsessed with "figuring things out," seeking knowledge constantly, or attempting to teach others at every turn while neglecting their own source of sacred truth: the heart. A female example of the Cryptic Sage would be Professor Trelawney in Harry Potter. A tortoise example is Master Oogway from Kung Fu Panda. Even Yoda leans toward the Cryptic side.

Where the Dogmatic Sage is redeemed through truth-telling, the Cryptic Sage is redeemed through clarity-seeking. Where the Dogmatic Sage wants to be right, the Cryptic Sage is afraid of being wrong. The Cryptic Sage hesitates to choose a path of action because they must analyze each and every possible path out of fear of choosing a less-than-best option. And yes, it's giving, "If you're not first, you're last, Ricky Bobby," but with nerds. Most of the time, the Cryptic Sage has an advanced intellect, with superior pattern recognition skills and strong intuition. They often feel misunderstood, but fail to realize their own lack of clarity and humility is contributing to that dynamic. It's not that they're being intentionally obtuse— it's that their egos have filled their minds with thoughts, facts, rules, arguments, and speculations to a point where it's a whole disorganized mess. It's hard to articulate a clear truth when the brain is swirling with chaotic knowledge! The first step in any organization effort — including ones in the brain — is to learn how to surrender the clutter and strip down to the truth.

Gandalf from The Lord of the Rings is a beautiful example of this journey from confusion to clarity. When we meet Gandalf the Grey, he only ever offers Cryptic hints and indirect warnings to the Hobbits on their journey ("Keep it secret, keep it safe"). He knows too much, and says too little. He largely operates this way out of fear of the Ring itself and his knowledge of how it corrupts almost everyone who touches it. Later on (spoiler alert), when he sacrifices himself, faces cosmic evil, and resurrects as Gandalf the White, he becomes clear and decisive, laser focused on completing his mission to unite the Free Peoples of Middle-Earth. This process, sometimes called "ego disintegration," is a big part of the redemption of the Sage. Gandalf described the experience as, "Then the darkness took me; and I strayed out of thought and time... Naked, I was sent back..." Isn't that interesting? The phrase "strayed out of thought and time" indicates that Gandalf had to surrender his thoughts, to let them go, to detach from the world he thought he knew. When he describes himself as being sent back "naked," that tells us he was stripped of the ego, of fear, of identity, of analysis, so that only truth remained.

The process of "ego disintegration" does not have to include such a dramatic event as death and resurrection, though. Devoting oneself to meditation practice is just as effective, and a lot less intimidating. The goal of meditation is to quiet the mind and place the ego in check. You've probably heard of "yoga" (unless you live under a rock), but if you're in the West, you probably also associate yoga with bendy blonde women rapidly shifting through stretches while wearing spandex in an exercise class setting that may or may not be 100 degrees on purpose. When I studied to become a yoga teacher, I learned that couldn't be further from the origins and history of yoga.

Yoga, especially Ashtanga yoga, was designed by men, for men, not as a way to get physically fit, but as a way to get mentally and spiritually fit. The poses are just one of eight "branches" of the complete practice. The first two branches deal with getting your heart clear by abstaining from certain immoral things (e.g. violence, stealing, lying) and adopting habits and attitudes that support harmony and clarity (e.g. cleanliness, self-discipline, surrender). The third branch includes the physical poses that are meant to help you free the mind from disturbances caused by stiffness or blockages in your physical body. The fourth branch is about learning to control the breath. The fifth teaches you to open and close your physical senses. The sixth is concentration, the seventh is meditation, and the eighth is bliss or oneness and dissolution of ego. The Yoga Sutras by a man named Patanjali describes these steps in great detail, if you're interested.

Walking the path of yoga helps the Sage gain clarity and courage through the releasing of mental clutter, as well as humility and detachment from dogma through the revival of wonder and curiosity. It is the most intelligent Sages who have the hardest time learning to meditate, despite being most in need of it. The more "cerebral" you are, the harder it will be to surrender the constant stream of thoughts flooding your mind. The 8 branches of yoga help slow-walk you into being able to meditate by starting with addressing some of the reasons you might have cognitive clutter in the first place (e.g. guilt, regret, conflict, anxiety, pain) so that when you get to branch 7, you can truly get out of your own head and your own way.

When the Sage does reach the 8th branch of "Samadhi" (oneness) they become free from both thoughts and time, just as Gandalf said. They experience a different way of knowing the truth through clarity of being, something Robert Wolff describes in his book Original Wisdom. Moreover, they recover a sense of awe and wonder that is devoid in the Dogmatic Sage who thinks he knows it all and can outsmart any opponent and is diminished in the Cryptic Sage for whom overthinking brings fear or frantic energy.

In a deep meditative state, you realize that there truly is nothing to fear but fear itself, and instead, you just feel in awe. You understand that life is so much bigger than your single human experience, and the feeling of being relatively insignificant is a relief, actually, a weight of expectations lifted from your shoulders. Like the quote I used from Socrates at the beginning of the chapter, the feeling of knowing nothing is the root of true wisdom. When you experience this level of clarity, it's much harder to be arrogant and much easier to become curious, almost like being reborn free from all the knowledge and beliefs instilled into you in your lifetime. This practice helps the Sage stop over-analyzing and choose to walk in truth with wisdom and faith.

When we examine Jesus as a divine Sage, we find he was well-known for fasting, praying, and meditating alone with God and for never letting his head overrule his heart. He personified truth-telling, but often spoke to people in parables. When his disciples asked him about why he chose to teach with stories in this way, he explained that while they (the disciples) might understand the plain-spoken truth, it would only confuse those with less spiritual experience. By speaking in parables, Jesus was able to deliver hard, complex, or controversial truths in a way the majority of people could clearly comprehend, contemplate, and retell.

He carefully crafted paradoxes, like in the Sermon on the Mount, to help free people from Dogmatic thinking through wonder and curiosity. Imagine hearing Jesus tell the crowd (paraphrasing): "It is easier for a camel to pass through the eye of a needle than for a rich man to enter Heaven." This message would have been both shocking (wonder-inspiring, perhaps even laughter-inspiring) and yet crystal clear in its meaning. Introducing clear and profound truth in a way that disarms the ego-resistance of the audience and causes them to wonder and reflect is the hallmark of the divine Sage.

Benjamin Franklin provides a more recent historical representation of the Sage, but with similar flare for parable and metaphor. You may recall that Franklin published a yearly magazine called "Poor Richard's Almanack" where he penned all kinds of general wisdom and clever, digestible nuggets of truth. But you may not know that he was the originator of some of our most common modern axioms, like "no pain, no gain" and "well done is better than well said" and "haste makes waste." He also valued honesty as a critical virtue, coining the phrase: honesty is the best policy.

In his essay "On Truth and Falsehood" published in 1730, Franklin wrote, "There can be no excuse for lying, neither is there anything equally despicable and dangerous as a liar, no man being safe who associates with him; for he who will lie will swear to it, says the proverb; and such a one may endanger my life, turn my family out of doors, and ruin my reputation, whenever he shall find it his interest!" Later on in the same essay he describes truth as "the companion of the gods, the joy of heaven, the light of the earth, the pedestal of justice, and the basis of good policy," and, "the centre on which all things rested: a chart to sail by, a remedy for all evils, and a light to the whole world." Benjamin Franklin was a Sage who understood that truth was his greatest ally and deception his greatest foe.

For another modern example of the nontoxic Sage, check out Carl Sagan's work. Even if you disagree with some of the ideas he expresses (like the theory of evolution), you still have to admit that he was masterful at communicating wisdom with great clarity. He once wrote, "The dangers of not thinking clearly are much greater now than ever before. It's not that there's something new in our way of thinking - it's that credulous (believable but perhaps untrue) and confused thinking can be much more lethal in ways it was never before." He went on to say, "The truth may be puzzling. It may take some work to grapple with. It may be counterintuitive. It may contradict deeply held prejudices. It may not be consonant with what we desperately want to be true. But our preferences do not determine what's true." There is a lesson here for every Sage.

You shall know the truth, and the truth shall set you free.

Reflection

Get ready to take the stage, Sage! It is the responsibility of the Sage to bring clarity, truth, and curiosity to lift the world out of confusion, deception, and dogma. Before you hop on a plane to India to visit a yoga ashram, let's pause to reflect on how you can unburden your inner Sage right where you are:

- What is the biggest barrier to truth-telling in your life: fear, arrogance, or lack of clarity? How can you take steps to address and overcome this barrier?
- What is one belief you hold or thought that you persistently think that is based in lies rather than in truth? What is the actual truth according to your heart?
- If silent, seated meditation is not really your cup of tea, have you considered journaling as a way to collect and organize your thoughts outside of your head, as a way to bring clarity to what is true versus what is assumption or speculation?

Chapter Summary

- Theme: Wisdom and Truth
- Key to Growth: Curiosity and Clarity
- Essence: The Sage seeks truth to be able to enlighten others. This archetype is grounded in lifelong wondering and curiosity.
- Pitfall to Avoid: Overthinking and dogma
- Growth Focus: Disciplining the ego to prioritize the heart; gaining clarity through stillness and surrender

9

The Explorer

Overview

- **Description:** The Explorer embodies discovery, adventure, and the desire for freedom. He is the archetype of autonomy and the pursuit of novelty.
- **Major Conflict:** The Explorer struggles with the balance between wanderlust and commitment. He risks becoming either a restless Escapist or a disillusioned Drifter.
- **Path to Growth:** The Explorer becomes his best self by finding meaning and gratitude in his journeys and embracing commitment.

Stories of the Explorer

> "I would rather die of passion than of boredom." – Vincent van Gogh

Ahoy, mateys, hoist the colors! We have arrived at the pirates chapter at last! I'm being silly but also serious. From Odysseus to Indiana Jones, from Captain Nemo to Captain Jack Sparrow, the Explorer archetype is probably the second most celebrated masculine archetype, next to the Hero, yet it is also one of the most misunderstood. In

fact, I would say that in our collective stories, the toxic Explorers far
outnumber the nontoxic ones. But at present, the world needs men
who dare to discover, who push boundaries, who bring back stories
and novelties that expand our understanding. These are the Explorers.

Two of my favorite nontoxic Explorers are Rhett McLaughlin and
Link Neal from the popular Youtube series Good Mythical Morning. Rhett and Link specialize in exploring a whole variety of topics
and experiences ranging from bizarre food tasting to testing full-body
airbags meant to cushion a fall (spoiler: that's one of the funniest
videos in the world.) They understand the strength of the Explorer:
novelty-induced delight. A novelty is simply something you've never
seen or experienced before, and it creates a sense of wonder or pleasure in you as you discover it. Every day Rhett and Link commit
themselves to demonstrating something new and unexpected to delight their audience and fulfill the need we all have to discover. This
is the gift of the Explorer.

Consider Joe Rogan as the Explorer. Instead of going out into the
world exploring, Joe brings the world into his studio. The lesson he
models for other Explorers is how to achieve a deep level of commitment - to his family, friends, work, and even to his own body
through training - while also maintaining freedom (autonomy) and
creating an environment just chocked full of novelty to explore and
share with others. Rogan is an Explorer of consciousness, of the unknown, of the mysterious. He's told stories of exploration through
unorthodox physical means — like meditating in a "float tank" (also
called "sensory deprivation tank") or experimenting with psychoac-
tive substances, and importantly, he recalls these experiences without
shame, fully embracing that exploration is his role and there is nothing wrong with that. In fact, it's deeply masculine.

Part of the reason for the success of Good Mythical Morning
(GMM) and the Joe Rogan Experience (JRE) podcast is that viewers
go there "expecting the unexpected" (to steal a phrase from Oscar
Wilde) - you never know what new ideas or stories will be discovered

that might completely boggle your mind (novelty). The JRE conversations run deep and hold space for a lot of nuance and grappling with concepts. He shows sincere gratefulness not only for his guests but also for his job - his ability to share thought-provoking and mind-freeing discussions with others. The GMM guys are equally gracious and have different themes, but with the same level of novelty as JRE. It's not lost on me that Joe Rogan used to host Fear Factor, which in some ways was a precursor to some of Rhett and Link's taste-tests!

It will probably come as no surprise that the main struggle for the Explorer is commitment, so let's talk about that briefly. You've probably heard the old trope that men have "commitment issues" or "fear of commitment" more than women do. Maybe you've even heard that men are "biologically wired" to wander from place to place, person to person to "spread their seed" far and wide. But did you know all that is a bunch of hooey? There is not strong scientific evidence that men are significantly more likely than women to have commitment issues! In fact, almost all the evidence points to the contrary - that women and men are equally likely to want to get married and "settle down" rather than "playing the field." Back when only husbands could file for divorce and controlled much of the wealth and property, it was true that men left their wives more than wives left their husbands, but now women are much more likely to initiate divorce than men. In fact, men benefit greatly, perhaps even more than women, from being in long-term committed relationships in terms of happiness, health, wealth, and longevity.

We can thank mainstream evolutionary psychology for this propaganda that men have evolved to be especially promiscuous while women evolved to be especially monogamous. The works of David Buss and others in this field pitched human sexuality as highly competitive, jealous, and possessive by nature, much like chimpanzees. They basically created a blanket excuse for male infidelity, abandonment, and domestic violence based in jealousy (a.k.a. "mate-guarding") as "natural." But recent authors have challenged this narrative.

In their book Sex at Dawn, researchers Christopher Ryan and Cacilda Jethá propose that it's capitalist patriarchy, especially in its creation of father-to-son inheritance systems, that has created this tense sexual environment, not nature. They criticize the mainstream theories for relying too heavily on studying chimpanzees, who are quite promiscuous, jealous, and even abusive, while ignoring other primates who don't act like that at all, like bonobos, gorillas, or gibbons. They claim that patterns of jealousy and fidelity (or lack thereof) are entirely culturally constructed, and that what is natural is for people to form multiple healthy committed relationships (romantic and not) in order to have a prosperous, harmonious tribe and society. Anthropologists like Christopher Boehm and even neuroscientists like Cordelia Fine have further disputed the mainstream evolutionary scientists' claims that men's brains are "wired" for wandering, supporting the idea that men and women desire strong bonds with their partners, family, and community at almost equal rates.

Now that we've cleared the air on that, let's discuss that small percentage of men (and women) who do have fear of commitment: the toxic Escapist Explorer. The unwillingness to commit in relationships, or even in occupations or hobbies, usually comes from a childhood abandonment wound. The abandoned inner child has a very hard time trusting others and therefore committing to relationships. But when we view this through the lens of the Explorer, that fear of commitment becomes the fear of "being tied down." The Explorer, more than anything, wants to be free to roam, unchained and untethered. They long for novelty - new sights, new experiences, new people with new stories. The Escapist idolizes novelty, worships it even, to the point that he prioritizes evading most if not all forms of routine and commitment, seeing roots as shackles.

The passion for novelty is not a flaw of the Explorer; it's a feature. Novelty is one of the universal human needs, and no one knows how to deliver it like an Explorer. Toxicity begins to creep in when the Escapist Explorer starts believing that commitment is the antithesis of novelty. Among toxic explorers who self-report as "commitment-phobic" three fourths described the fear of abandonment as a top reason for being resistant to commit, but four fifths said they were afraid of being stuck with the "wrong person." This hearkens back to decades-old discourse about marriage being "boring" because a man "has to sleep with the same woman every night." These ideas exaggerate the lack of novelty within committed relationships and frankly, terrify the Escapist Explorer who starts feeling trapped by even the possibility of monotony and routine.

Jack Sparrow from the Pirates of the Caribbean films is a prime example of the Escapist Explorer. Not only is he quite literally an escape artist when it comes to evading enforcers of the law, but also he clearly struggles with commitment, even to his own word. One of the funniest scenes of Captain Jack happens on the Island of Tortuga when multiple women accost him in a row for presumably "loving-and-leaving" them in his endless quest for freedom and exploration of the open seas. "I probably deserved that," is one of my favorites of all his lines in that movie, second only to: "I wash my hands of this weirdness."

It paints a curious picture that the only person to ever truly trap Jack Sparrow was one of the people he was most committed to: Elizabeth Swann. But in that moment when she handcuffs him to the mast to save the crew and abandons him to death by Kraken, he accepts her choice and his consequences, plunging into the Explorer's worst nightmare: Davy Jones' Locker - a time-loop purgatory almost like Groundhog Day but with sand dunes, rock-crabs, Jack Sparrow clones and not much else. Talk about lack of novelty!

The way out of this particular toxicity is to lean in. In the words of Captain Jack Sparrow himself, "The problem is not the problem. The problem is your attitude about the problem." If you have the attitude that committed relationships are a ball-and-chain, then you'll have problems with connection, intimacy, and commitment. But if you change your attitude and decide that commitments strengthen your adventures by at the very least providing you someone to share them with, those problems begin to dissipate. Every ship needs an anchor, right? In the end, what redeemed Jack was his willingness to sacrifice eternal freedom as captain of the Flying Dutchman because he was more committed to his friends. "Not all treasure is silver and gold, mate," he reminds us. People you can rely on and share life's joys and trials with, who won't give up on you and will love you for who you are - that's the real treasure every Explorer seeks, whether or not they are ready to admit it.

The second toxic version of the Explorer is the disillusioned Drifter. The Drifter is not as well documented in our collective stories as the Escapist, but he's still present. Instead of actively exploring, the Drifter takes a passive approach and just goes where the winds of change take him, often avoiding conflict as well as deep connection, commitment, or intimacy through indecision and "shrugging off". Anthony Bourdain is an example of the Explorer who leaned toward the disillusioned Drifter. In spite of his many adventures and experiences with novelty, Bourdain carried a heart heavy with disillusionment that no amount of exploration could quite lift. The word "disillusionment" is defined as "disappointment that something is not as good in reality as you imagined it would be," but literally it means, "to have broken the illusion". The Drifter often starts by believing the illusion that life is going to be better or more exciting just around the next river bend. His exploits center less around escaping others and more around escaping his own discontent and boredom. When he realizes no amount of exploration seems to help him find the thrill he seeks, he becomes cynical and indifferent. "Nothing is new under the sun," eh?

In order to let go of the toxicity of disillusionment, the Drifter needs to face his grief and release comparison. The Escapist is held in toxicity by unresolved fear, but the Drifter is held in toxicity by unresolved loss. When someone has unresolved loss (grief), they very often get stuck in a cycle of comparison, absolutism, and hypotheticals. Let me give you some examples of what this sounds like. Read the following list of statements, and see if you or someone you love has ever expressed something similar:

- "This would be better if X were here..."
- "Life was better before X happened..."
- "Things will never be the same now..."
- "I'll never be able to find the same love/joy..."
- "Some people are just more lucky than others..."
- "I'll always be missing a piece of myself now..."
- "Things were better in the past..."
- "If only I had X, I'd be happy..."
- "I wish I could go back in time..."

Those are all statements of someone with unresolved loss. Many of these statements are comparing the uncomfortable present to the idealized past, but in all of them, they're describing a fantasy and not a fact. For example, there's no guarantee that life would be any better or any worse if a loss did not occur. If you think about it, almost every single movie about time traveling teaches us that even if we could change the past, it wouldn't necessarily result in a better future! The disillusioned Drifter is almost always judging the present as inferior to the past or judging the experiences of others as superior to his own. Exploration no longer meets his expectations because grief has dulled his senses. He feels like swimming upstream would be pointless, and so he just drifts along wherever the current takes him, despondent, disconnected, just going through the motions.

To face grief, first we have to pinpoint exactly what it was we lost that broke our illusion that life was somehow going to be better or different than how it currently is in reality. When the loss is a person who died, that's fairly easy to pinpoint, but there are other losses that deeply affect men, like the loss of a job, of a marriage, of a home, or even of a dream. You can also lose trust, lose respect, lose faith, and lose face. Any time you experience loss, there is grief there. For Anthony Bourdain I can only speculate, but I imagine he lost hope in humanity every time he was out exploring the world and compared the suffering of the many to the opulence of a few.

Once we've pinpointed what we've lost, we need to figure out what story we are telling ourselves about that loss and question that narrative-loop. Maybe the story is, "It's not fair!" In the words of William Goldman in The Princess Bride, "Who said life is fair? Where is that written?" Another popular story we tell ourselves is, "I'll never be the same." But… Aren't we always changing? Are we ever the exact same as we were in the past? Will we be the same in ten years as we are today? Another common grief-loop is some version of regret that sounds like, "If only I had done X then I wouldn't have lost Y." How can you be so certain of that? What if you did X and then lost Y another way? This kind of logic exercise helps us dispel the fallacies that we've allowed to fester in our minds and create feelings of disappointment and despair.

Remember what Rafiki said to Simba in The Lion King, "The past can hurt. But the way I see it, you can either run from it or learn from it." To learn from loss, we need to replace our toxic story about the loss with a meaningful and empowering one instead. Simba's toxic story was "Hakuna Matata" - which means, "No worries," but essentially meant an avoidance of life's problems, embracing a life of drifting and avoiding commitment after the traumatic loss of his father, Mufasa. The meaningful story he chose to replace Hakuna Matata was, "He (Mufasa) lives in me (Simba)." When you believe that your loved ones live on in your heart, it eases the pain of separation from them and gives you more incentive to honor their memory (meaning). When you focus on what makes you feel grateful about the people or things you have lost, you attract more people and things into your life to fill that void. Gratitude is a tonic for grief.

When I was young, I knew and loved an Explorer named John K. Phillips. John was a veteran Airman with the United States Air Force who became a cross-country truck driver when he returned to civilian life. He was intensely committed to his family, neighbors, and church. He was masterful at telling tales of his explorations, near and far, and every time I heard his rig pull up outside the church, I would smile. He was also a gift-giver, which was a little bit fitting since he kind of looked like a younger, taller version of Santa Claus with the same rosy cheeks and twinkle in his bespectacled eyes. Over the years that I had the pleasure to know him, he brought me every flavor of Symphony chocolate bar that could be found across the US, and on more than one occasion he showed up with dozens of boxes of roses that he scavenged from a big-box flower distributor's dumpsters that happened to be next to one of his drop off points.

It was John who inspired me to become a floral designer with his love of beauty and novelty. But John's life was not all chocolate and roses. He experienced tremendous tragedy and grief when he was widowed as a young adult and then again when one of his sons passed away suddenly. He could have easily become the disillusioned Drifter, but instead he focused on honoring the memory of those he lost through loving and caring for his friends and family who were still here.

Indiana Jones is another Explorer who tends toward the Drifter, even though he escaped his fair number of scrapes! He becomes disillusioned throughout the films because he keeps losing his archaeological relics to actual villains to be used selfishly or violently. His nemesis Belloq in the Raiders of the Lost Ark famously taunted him: "Again we see there is nothing you can possess which I cannot take away." Talk about a toxic story of loss that might get stuck in someone's head!

But in the film, The Last Crusade, we see young Indy receive an interesting piece of advice after he loses the Cross of Coronado: "You lost today kid, but that doesn't mean you have to like it." The message here is: loss must be accepted, but you get to decide how you respond to that loss. Do you give up, become a bitter Drifter? Or do you dust yourself off and get back to exploring? Do you decide to be grateful for the good times and the bad? The choice is yours. It's also fun to note that Indiana Jones and Jack Sparrow are both redeemed in the end by the same thing: their recognition that family and friends are the real treasure worth keeping.

If you'd like more examples of nontoxic Explorers, look no further than Star Trek with James T. Kirk and Jean-Luc Picard. Captain Kirk's shadow is the Escapist and Captain Picard's shadow is the Drifter. One interesting note of contrast between Kirk and Picard is that Kirk focuses on external exploration and novelty - finding new planets, new species, new adventures; whereas, Picard focuses on internal exploration and novelty - finding new ways of thinking about old problems, new ethical considerations, new feelings. Both characters face tremendous loss — Kirk loses his son (murdered by Klingons) and his best friend Spock (who sacrificed himself to save the starship Enterprise); Picard loses his brother and nephew (in a tragic fire) and himself (when he is assimilated by the Borg). Both of them are redeemed from their toxic sides through commitment to their crews and resolving their losses, but also finding a deep sense of gratitude for all the experiences they collected through the episodes.

Even Jesus of Nazareth can be seen through the lens of the Explorer. That guy was always on the move! But much like Captain Picard or Joe Rogan, the main explorations of Jesus were internal - in the hearts of his disciples and followers. He was not afraid to do things no one had done (like heal people on the Sabbath, turn water into wine) or say things no one had ever said before (like "the kingdom of God is within you" or "the first shall be last"). This is philosophical novelty. This is exploration on a deep spiritual level. It's a brilliant example of how the Explorer grows through sharing novelties and being committed to others as much as they are committed to discovery and adventure.

Reflection

There are so many Explorers that didn't get mentioned in this chapter, but I guess you'll have to just go on an exploration of your own to find out more because I'm reaching my page limit! In the meantime, consider the following questions to reflect on your own Explorer energy:

- How are you using exploration or adventure (internal or external) as a way to escape something or someone you're committed to in your life? What is one way that you can include them in your explorations and/or lean into your commitment to them instead?
- What loss have you experienced that still makes you want to take off or check out? How can you change your story around that loss in a way that adds meaning or purpose back to your life?
- Can you name 3 instances in your life where you felt profoundly grateful to have discovered something new? Now, can you share those stories with 3 people to inspire them? How did that make you feel?

Chapter Summary

- Theme: Adventure and Novelty
- Key to Growth: Commitment and Gratitude
- Essence: The Explorer thrives on new experiences, constantly seeking to expand their world and understand themselves. This archetype represents discovery and delight.
- Pitfall to Avoid: Restlessness, escapism, or disillusionment; unwillingness to commit or resolve one's grief
- Growth Focus: Finding meaning in the ups and downs, valuing commitment as something that complements freedom, and balancing exploration with rootedness.

10

The Innocent

Overview

- **Description:** The Innocent represents purity, optimism, faith and trust. He is the archetype of simplicity and the belief in the goodness of life.
- **Major Conflict:** The Innocent struggles with delusions and denial. He risks becoming either overly trusting and gullible (Fool) or faithless and paranoid (Victim).
- **Path to Growth:** The Innocent grows by maintaining faith while staying grounded in reality, becoming aware of and accepting hard truths, and inspiring others with his optimism.

Stories of the Innocent

> "Keep your face always toward the sunshine—and shadows will fall behind you." – Walt Whitman

If you've made it this far in this book then I probably don't have to tell you this, but "nice guys finish last" is a toxic masculine trope that serves the capitalist patriarchy. The idea that "real men" are cut-throat and cruel serves shareholders, not society at large. The archetype of the Innocent reminds us that it is deeply masculine to be pure of heart, optimistic, faithful, and trusting. Let's look at some really wholesome examples first.

Steve Irwin is probably my favorite real-life example of the Innocent. He was called "The Crocodile Hunter," but in some ways that was a misnomer because he wasn't hunting crocodiles as much as he was rescuing them. He had a heart of gold with a contagious, almost childlike enthusiasm for nature and creatures big and small. He always had a smile on his face and a twinkle in his eyes. One of his most memorable and perhaps revealing quotes was, "I have no fear of losing my life — if I have to save a koala or a crocodile or a kangaroo or a snake, mate, I will save it!" This shows the true masculine power of the Innocent: faithfulness and optimism.

Even though Steve Irwin was not a preacher in a religious sense, he displayed tremendous faith in the universe, which is why he wasn't worried about losing his own life — he had faith that everything would work out if he stayed true to his calling of educating people about endangered animals and habitat destruction. "I am optimistic globally," Irwin once said. "So many scientists are working frantically on the reparation of our planet." And he really believed that. He believed in and trusted the goodness in every living thing, even the scariest ones like crocodiles, vipers, and human beings. This is the positive energy of the Innocent.

A fictional example of the nontoxic Innocent is Samwise Gamgee from the Lord of the Rings. Sam is not the cleverest character in the Fellowship, nor is he the most ambitious. He is, however, the most good and pure of heart. He doesn't lust for glory, which is evident when he holds the Ring and is not seduced by its power. Instead Sam dreams of simple joys: gardens and good food, hobbit girls and shire sunsets. He stays optimistic and faithful to his friends in spite of their challenges and conflicts to the point where he physically carries Frodo in the end to complete their mission. He reminds us to keep believing in goodness, to keep hoping and having faith in ourselves, our friends, and our calling. "There's some good in the world, Mr. Frodo… and it's worth fighting for."

Samwise demonstrates how the Innocent is endowed with endurance, fueled by faith that good will overcome evil in the end. Their endurance is a result of not being weighed down by worry or fear because they have strong faith that everything will work itself out eventually. In Mark Chapter 10, Jesus elevates the Innocent archetype when he says: "Let the little children come to me, and do not hinder them, for the kingdom of God belongs to such as these. Truly I tell you, anyone who will not receive the kingdom of God like a little child (with full faith) will never enter it."

The Innocents seem childlike because they aren't burdened by an overbearing ego in the same way as other archetypes. Instead, they are pure-hearted and full of faith, which gives them an emotional clarity that others (like the Sage or Warrior) struggle to obtain. In fact, it is common for a Sage and an Innocent to be paired together as "foils" in stories so that they each have a lesson to teach the other. For example, Arthur and Merlin are Innocent and Sage in The Sword and the Stone animated film, where Arthur teaches Merlin how to release dogma and connect his heart to his head, and Merlin teaches Arthur how to be more skeptical and less gullible.

This leads us to one of the ways that the Innocent archetype can become toxic: the Fool. The Foolish Innocent is trusting to a fault. He is gullible and easily taken advantage of by craftier archetypes (looking at you, Magicians). The Fool and the Drifter have one major thing in common — they both have a hard time integrating past painful or traumatic events in a way that serves them well in the present. Where the Drifter battles bitterness and apathy, the Fool struggles with delusion (false beliefs) and denial. Have you ever heard of "toxic positivity"? That is a sure sign of the Fool!

Speaking of toxic positivity, let's look at a pop culture example of the Fool: Buddy the Elf. First, just take a minute to consider the amount of delusion and denial that Buddy maintained during almost the entire movie Elf. The most memorable example is when he believes so strongly that Miles (played by Peter Dinklage) is an elf (delusion) that he continues to deny the evidence that Miles does not, in fact, identify as an elf. "Oh, he's an **angry** elf!" Buddy exclaims as Miles lunges at him violently.

Now think about what was driving Buddy's behavior: an abandonment wound - just like we talked about in the previous chapter. Buddy had childlike faith in the goodness of everyone around him, which was challenged right away when he found himself surrounded by New Yorkers. His identity as an elf is based in fantasy (delusion) even though it's obvious by his size that he doesn't belong at the North Pole. He has even more delusions about what humans, namely his father, will be like and how they will spend their time together (e.g. eating cookie dough, holding hands, snuggling). He refuses to recognize (denial) that his father and other humans are rejecting him and all his Christmas cheer. Instead of taking the many hints, he doubles down on his performative positivity.

In the end, Buddy becomes redeemed through awareness and acceptance of hard truths. All Fools must face the music. They must have their "I've been a fool" moment of reckoning. Otherwise it's hard to break the delusions. In a scene of quiet desperation, Buddy goes to the bridge and looks over the edge, saying, "I don't belong anywhere..." This is rock bottom. What stops Buddy from "losing faith" and jumping is his Sage shows up — Santa — and he needs Buddy's help to fix his sleigh! Santa, with his gift of converting confusion to clarity, helps Buddy become aware of his unique identity - not as human OR elf, but as human AND elf.

Buddy sets off to save the day, no longer the Fool he once was. He helps Jovie face her stage fright without invalidating her fear (denial) or overwhelming her with toxic positivity (delusion), and instead he imbues her with a gentle, realistic optimism and has faith in her and in the Christmas Spirit. He learns to accept that not everyone is on the Nice List and that "good" things (like cheer or maple syrup) are only truly good and appreciated in the right context. This is redemption of the Fool.

Forrest Gump is another nontoxic example of the Innocent. Forrest is gullible and loyal to a fault, but he is no Fool. When his childhood girlfriend Jenny rejected his marriage proposal, he accepted her answer and didn't retreat into denial. Instead he questions her and shows his own self-awareness. "Why don't you love me, Jenny? I'm not a smart man," admits Forrest, "but I know what love is." Remember how the Innocent has endurance because they aren't weighed down by ego? This is perfectly portrayed in Forrest's running across America journey.

Forrest Gump's optimism and faith shines throughout his relationships, where he sees the good in his friends even when they are acting badly. In the scene where he finds out he's the father of Jenny's son, we see more of Forrest's awareness and lack of delusion as he begins to panic and asks Jenny if the boy is smart or... like himself. He is visibly relieved when she tells him little Forrest is the smartest boy in the class. Forrest Gump is one of the purest-hearted characters in all of cinema, and by enduring the bullying, rejection, and tragedy life threw into his box of chocolates with acceptance and faithfulness, he shows us the quiet nobility of the Innocent.

The second version of the toxic Innocent is the Victim. Where the Fool leans toward delusions of grandeur and positivity, the Victim leans toward delusions of paranoia and self-pity. They operate from a world view that everyone and everything is out to get them, that only bad things ever happen to them, and/or that they must be cursed. This is also a form of "losing faith" just like we saw with Buddy. Think Eeyore from Winnie the Pooh, Charlie Brown from Peanuts, or even George Costanza from Seinfeld. They've falsely believed that what happens to them defines them. "That's just my luck!" Charlie Brown says with a sigh as Lucy pulls the football away for the 100th time. That's not luck, Charlie Brown. That's denial and delusion on your part, my guy.

The Victim is in denial about their own agency. My own father has a lot of the traits of the Innocent (no wonder his favorite Christmas movie is Elf, right?). When my brother and I were young, he continually taught us to not give away our agency to victimhood and blaming. I mentioned this in the Warrior chapter too, but Dad would repeat axioms like, "No one makes you mad. You make yourself mad," or the more popular, "It takes two to tango/argue." He also taught us that we cannot control others; we can only ever control how we react to others. The rules in our house were clear: do obey God, do honor your parents, and do unto others as you would have them do to you; don't disobey, don't defy, and don't disrespect. If we broke the rules, there were consequences, and we had no one to blame but ourselves. This produced a strong sense of agency in us because we knew exactly what not to do but also exactly what TO DO.

The Innocent slips easily into toxic victimhood because they don't fully understand what to do. It's like it really is their first rodeo. To take back their own power, they need to explore and assert their agency. The Latin root word "agentia" simply means "doer" or "one who does." Personal agency, then, is our free will, our power to do whatever we choose. The toxic Victim Innocent believes they are powerless with no agency, a helpless soul, caught in the crossfire of tragic circumstances and "bad people" with nowhere to go and nothing that can be done. Sometimes they blame themselves for what has happened to them. Because they are deeply naive yet full of faith, sometimes they believe God is punishing them or that he wants them to punish themselves through martyrdom. Other times they believe if they passively suffer in silence long enough (toxic endurance), God will eventually save them. This is all delusion.

There's an old parable that says: a preacher was stranded on his roof during a terrible flood and he prayed to God to save him. Then a canoe passed by, and the paddlers called out to rescue the preacher, and he replied, "Go on and pick up someone else! God will save me!" The waters rose and the preacher continued to pray, then a motorboat passed by, and the drivers urged the man of God to get onboard. He still called back, "Go on and pick up someone else! God will save me!" The waters continued to rise as the preacher continued to pray for salvation. Then a helicopter flew over and dropped a rope ladder down to him. "Go on!" He shouted. "God will save me!" Then the preacher drowned, and when he got to the pearly gates he looked at the Lord and said, "I had complete faith in you. Why didn't you save me?" And God said, "Rev, I sent you two boats and a helicopter. What more do you want from me?" This is a picture of the full-of-faith but also deeply naive Victim. Faith alone is not enough to save us. We must also DO something, even if it's simply accepting help in a time of need.

The hard truth for the Innocent Victim to accept is: God rains on the just (good) and the unjust (bad). God is not an interventionist - he's a consequentialist. He tells us we will reap what we sow. In the book of James he says, "Faith, without works is dead... by works a man is justified, not by faith alone." This is a message straight to the ears of the Innocent archetype saying: don't just believe (have faith) in good, DO GOOD; don't just believe things will get better, MAKE THINGS BETTER. Have enough faith to back it up with actions that you can be proud of, that uplift and encourage others to have hope even in the darkest days.

By playing the role of Victim, people give up their power to DO something to bring more good into their own lives and essentially allow their past to control their future. Victims must choose to rewrite their story as, "Yes, someone hurt or fooled me, but that is on them, and what is on me is: how I respond, where I go from here, what lesson I learn to help keep me safe moving forward, and who I share my story with to inspire them toward optimism." Victims need to accept that yes, sometimes bad things do happen to good people, but good people can also create space and boundaries between themselves and "bad people" and still be good and faithful and true to their pure hearts. You can still give people the benefit of the doubt and see the good in them while protecting yourself from their harmful actions by actually DOING something to change your situation and create boundaries. Don't just pray for God to save you if you're not willing to move from your roof.

In the words of GWB, "Fool me once, shame on you; fool me twice? You won't fool me again." We have the agency to control who we trust and who we don't. Trusting liars is not a badge of faith -

it's a badge of foolishness. But fortunately, since we have agency over our own selves, there's always something we can do to shift our stories from victim to victor, to break the cycle of trauma, deception, or abuse. It may not always be clear — that's why the Innocent benefits from the Sage, to bring this clarity — but there will always be something you can do to reclaim your power and escape victim status.

Aang from Avatar: The Last Airbender is a nontoxic Innocent archetype who leans toward the Victim shadow. He has an abandonment wound that cuts both ways — where he feels abandoned by his tribe but also feels he abandoned them. The story he tells himself is that none of the trauma in his life would have happened if he hadn't run away from his responsibility as the Avatar. He blames himself and believes he's a failure, doomed to disappoint and hurt others even though that's not his intention. This is a false belief (delusion) that Aang must confront and change to become the mature and healthy version of the Innocent.

Aang overcomes the Victim shadow in the end through awareness and acceptance. He shifts his inner story about himself from broken failure (victim) to strong survivor (victor). He becomes aware of his own agency and accepts that the greatest failure is doing nothing and expecting things to change. He stops asking, "What if I fail?" and starts asking, "What can I do?" He leaves behind the identity of "the last Airbender" and steps into the identity of "the Avatar," the bridge between benders, pure of heart, full of faith and power.

It's been a while since we explored an event in world history inspired by one of the archetypes, so let's roll back the clock to 1914 - Christmas Eve to be exact. (Yes, I know, Buddy would be stoked about this story.) World War I had begun that summer, and already the Western Front was embroiled in brutal trench warfare - muddy, freezing, bloody, and unmoving. The British and German troops faced off across a no-man's-land of barbed wire, shell craters, and frozen corpses. Morale (optimism, faith) was low on both sides.

But just when they thought all faith was lost, the spirit of the Innocent appeared. German soldiers began lighting candles to decorate a makeshift Christmas tree in their trench. Then they started singing Silent Night. When the British soldiers heard them, they started singing along in English. In a few minutes, trust and faith began to flood over the soldiers as they emerged from their bunkers and crossed the no-man's-land to shake hands with their "enemies," exchange gifts with each other, and help bury and honor the fallen on both sides.

The Christmas Truce shows the true masculine power of the Innocent and maybe even shows why this archetype has been mostly mocked in modern media. The military industrial complex knows they'd never stand a chance if the Innocents understood their true power to restore faith and goodness to humanity.

Reflection

Switching gears from the Innocent to the Rebel (next chapter) might just give you whiplash from how opposite they are, so before we do a 180, let's reflect on how to encourage your inner Innocent:

- To be "pure of heart" means to be in alignment with goodness at every level of your being. Try speaking the following prayer for 30 days and see how it impacts your emotional clarity: Let my mind think good thoughts. Let my eyes see good in the world. Let my mouth speak good words. Let my heart feel good feelings. Let my hands do good work. Let my feet take me to good places. If you're like my dad, you can also break out into song a la James Brown, "I feel good, I knew that I would!"
- Consider where in your belief structure are you holding onto delusions (false beliefs - negative or positive)? What is a truth that needs to be accepted instead?
- How can you bring optimism and faith to others through sharing your story or perspective?

Chapter Summary

- Theme: Faith and Optimism
- Key to Growth: Awareness and Acceptance
- Essence: The Innocent archetype represents purity, faith, and optimism. This archetype believes in the good in others and inspires others to be better.
- Pitfall to Avoid: Naive delusions or denial of reality
- Growth Focus: Cultivating awareness and agency while maintaining trust, accepting the truth that nothing/no one is entirely good or entirely bad, uplifting others through optimism, faith, and endurance.

11

The Rebel

Overview

- **Description:** The Rebel is the archetype of revolution, non-conformity, and change. He challenges the status quo and fights for freedom and individuality.
- **Major Conflict:** The Rebel struggles with the balance between restriction and cooperation. He risks becoming either the rebel-without-a-cause (Anarchist) or quietly subversive and sabotaging (Dissident).
- **Path to Growth:** The Rebel becomes his best self by channeling his energy into constructive change, standing up for justice, and inspiring others to think differently.

Stories of the Rebel

"Rebellion against tyrants is obedience to God." – Benjamin Franklin

The Rebel might be my personal favorite masculine archetype. That's why I married one.... and he's a Capricorn to boot. (That's a niche joke, but if you know, you know.) My husband hates when I tell stories about him, so I'll just say I knew he was a Rebel from the moment he told me that as a child he would rage-chomp his communion wafers. Take that, body of Christ! But seriously, the hallmark of the Rebel is his unwillingness to conform or comply with unjust authority, unnecessary demands, or unwarranted restrictions on his freedom. To my husband as a twelve year old boy, being forced to attend Catholic mass met all three conditions for rebellion.

In the United States especially, we love to celebrate the Rebel because we are a nation built on rebellion. Just look at the Boston Tea Party - pure Rebel energy. Martin Luther King Jr. is also a prime example of a Rebel. Think about the Rebel's imperative: do not comply or conform to unjust authority, unnecessary demands, nor unwarranted restrictions of liberty. MLK easily recognized all three conditions for rebellion in the system of segregation and Jim Crow. Did you know he was arrested more than 30 times in his efforts to bring racial integration and equality to the United States?

Almost every Rebel archetype is subjected to some kind of captivity or detention, since it teaches them a lesson in liberation, which is their strength. While in the Birmingham jail, MLK penned profound philosophy on freedom and civil rights, including the Rebel's call to conscience: "One has a moral responsibility to disobey unjust laws." But he also wrote things that were highly controversial and challenged the status quo, like: "I have almost reached the regrettable conclusion that the Negro's great stumbling block... is not the Ku Klux Klanner, but the white moderate, who is more devoted to 'order' than to justice." This quote beautifully showcases the Rebel's ongoing conflict with the King archetype, who specializes in order but not necessarily liberty or justice, which is more in the Rebel's wheelhouse.

The person in my own life who best represents the nontoxic Rebel is my college roommate's brother Dr. Fady Joudah. The Joudah family was expelled from their home in Isdoud, Palestine during the Nakba of 1948. After moving around the Middle East as refugees, the family settled in the United States, while their extended family stayed behind in Gaza, the West Bank, and Jordan. As a result of their family's exile and continual restrictions, Fady and his siblings grew up in a household where prayers for the liberation of his people were offered up five times a day, where statelessness was faced with solidarity.

Fady Joudah went on to become a medical doctor, joining the organization Doctors Without Borders and working as a field doctor in Zambia and Sudan in the early 2000s. His missions took him into rural and resource-restricted areas that were highly affected by HIV/AIDS, malaria, and conflict. Ultimately his upbringing and his experiences led him to become a writer, poet, and translator of precious Palestinian poetry, such as the works of Mahmoud Darwish and Ghassan Zaqtan. Maybe you don't think that sounds very rebellious but consider that he chose to rebel against unjust occupation with a pen instead of a sword. In his work, he rebelled against the Western idea that Arabs and Palestinians, specifically, are somehow less valuable or more uncivilized than Americans or Europeans by sharing their stories of beauty, brilliance, and righteous resistance against unjust authority. "If we can't imagine a free liberated world in language, how can we build one?" Joudah once asked. This is a question for Rebels everywhere, especially since communication is an essential part of cooperation, which is the prime catalyst for growth in the Rebel.

We all know the Rebel, but what we don't seem to know is how to distinguish between what makes a Rebel toxic versus nontoxic. Instead we treat toxic Rebels as irredeemable, using cop-out phrases like: "That's just who they are." Like the King and the Sage, there are many men with the Rebel energy who are deemed "narcissists" because they have an overbearing ego and are at the same time driven by self-interest. They want to do what they want to do - regardless of the so-called "rules" or "laws," and they resent any kind of restrictions on their personal free will. They march to the beat of their own drum regardless of who gets hurt in the process.

This brings us to the first toxic type of the Rebel: the Anarchist. This toxic Rebel has a deep seated issue with authority. The Anarchist does not want to be told what to do or what not to do. You'll very often see conflict between the Rebel and the King types for this reason.

Anarchist Rebels view all rules as unnecessary restrictions, and prefer a system of governance that is ultra-libertarian, in which the inalienable rights to life, liberty, and the pursuit of happiness should not be infringed by any law. They're also what we call the "rebel-without-a-cause," meaning they rebel because they feel compelled to, with no real purpose or reasoning. They want to set fire to every system with no regard for the chaos that will ensue.

It's funny to me that political Anarchists like to set up businesses called "worker cooperatives" because the Anarchist archetype is quite possibly the hardest archetype to get to cooperate with anyone. They take the cake in terms of noncooperation through noncompliance. Even if they propose a plan, they may end up not complying with the plan later on if it suddenly feels too restrictive or if they just change their mind. And God forbid you make a demand of them instead of a request! That won't go over well at all. But at the end of the day, cooperation is the virtue that redeems the Rebel.

Let's look at Han Solo from Star Wars as an example of the Rebel who leans toward Anarchy. When we first meet Han, he's a smuggler who makes his own rules and frequently gets in trouble for noncompliance with deals he's made. Think about how much time and effort could have been saved if Han had simply paid his debts to Jabba the Hut, for instance. One of his most famous first lines is, "I ain't in this for your revolution, Princess. I expect to be well paid," but my personal favorite is, "Look, Your Worshipfulness, let's get one thing straight. I take orders from just one person: ME." That's the Anarchist Rebel.

Han Solo defiantly refuses to cooperate with plans, often causing unnecessary chaos and danger for himself and everyone else. Remember when he barreled into a room full of Storm Troopers in his attempt to rescue Leia? Or when he infuriated everyone by making a miraculous escape... into an even more perilous asteroid field? Good times! But in the end, he's redeemed when he decides that compliance and cooperation are not the same as conformity, the Rebel's greatest fear. You can still have free will and choose to use it to support your friends and family, rather than thwarting them with your bullheaded-ness.

Becoming a nontoxic Rebel doesn't mean that you have to aban-don the part of yourself that is defiant entirely, just that you have to choose what you rebel against or defy based on a cause like justice, love, or liberation of others. Rebel Jesus often defied the religious leaders of his time, challenging hypocrisy and injustice within reli-gious systems. In Mark Chapter 3, Jesus defies religious authorities by healing a man on the Sabbath, challenging rigid rules and prioritizing compassion over tradition. This act embodies the nontoxic Rebel's spirit of questioning norms, standing against unjust restrictions, and working to liberate others from oppression.

Regardless of how you feel about the guy, a modern day example of the Rebel is Elon Musk. Elon Musk embodies the Rebel archetype through his boundary-pushing approach in industries like space ex-ploration, electric vehicles, and tech innovation, but also in his per-sonal life with his unusually large number of children by different women and his proclivity for video games and psychedelic drugs. Un-conventional and willing to defy norms, Musk's vision challenges es-tablished ideas, driving change and inspiring others to think outside the box. Consider how many lawmakers (Kings) he upset with his "Department of Government Efficiency" program. Think about his later defiance and unwillingness to conform and cooperate with the Trump administration, with whom he had been in league for the first several months of Trump's second term. That's Elon's Anarchist Shadow making those memes at 2 a.m. y'all. Make no mistake.

The second way a Rebel slips into toxicity is by becoming the Dis-sident. Where the Anarchist sets fire to the system, the Dissident sets fire to himself to spite the system. Seething with rage just beneath the surface, his favorite word is: "NO," but when forced to cooperate, he schemes ways to sabotage others or plots quiet revenge against those who subjected him to even perceived restrictions. He speaks spitefully against anyone who conforms, calling them "sheeple," but most of his own rebellion is internalized as "rage against the machine" and not particularly visible to others. That is… until he snaps and moves from Dissident into something more akin to Terrorist.

The Dissident is the Rebel who resists not with loud bravado, but with secrets, solitude, and symbolism. V from the film V for Vendetta is a fictional example of the Dissident Rebel. The character V is deeply wounded. He was subjected to fascist imprisonment in a concentration camp, burned alive, and presumed dead. Until Evey came along, V lived alone with only books and music to keep him company while he schemed against the government from behind a mask. His tactics were subversive and sabotaging until the very end, when he went out with a literal bang. This story arc is both tragic and toxic, however noble V might have imagined his actions to be. In the end, he abandons Evey to die for his cause, unredeemed, but hoping he'll be redeemed in the next life. The Dissident Rebel is most often met with the "lost cause" mentality, but this doesn't have to be his fate.

The Dissident is redeemed by understanding that cooperation means working WITH someone, not FOR them — that cooperation is not subjugation. Read that again. The Dissident's secrecy must give way to solidarity. He must realize rebellion is more than resistance - it's a unifying and liberating force that requires cooperation with other people to create revolution and lasting change. If you're familiar with Cassian Andor from the Star Wars spin-off Andor, he is the Dissident who overcomes his shadow and rises in to the nontoxic Rebel in this very way. When we first meet Cassian he is self-interested and cynical, working for the Rebellion but not with them, per se.

By the Rogue One finale, Cassian has found his redemption through cooperation, connection, and cause. This is the healing of the Dissident Rebel, even though Cassian sacrifices his own life in the end, much like V. However unlike V and Evey, Cassian and Jyn make their final stand together, embracing each other after he tells her, "Your father would be proud of you, Jyn." Consider the difference between V who hides his plans from Evey out of fear that she will try to stop him versus Cassian who trusts Jyn fully, not just with the plan but with his whole heart. This is true cooperation for a cause, the salvation of the Rebel.

The truly nontoxic Rebel breaks chains without breaking hearts. He dismantles systems while upholding human dignity. He recognizes the difference between resistance and uprising. In India in 1930, the British crown imposed a heavy salt tax on Indian citizens and even criminalized them for collecting their own salt from the sea. In response, Mahatma Gandhi launched a 240 mile march from his ashram to the Arabian Sea. Thousands of people joined him and upon reaching the coast, they gathered salt, breaking the unjust law in full public view. Gandhi famously said it was, "civil disobedience, not civil war." This act of rebellion became a cornerstone of India's eventual independence from Britain and inspired other civil rights leaders like MLK.

Another historical example of the Dissident Rebel was Dietrich Bonhoeffer. Bonhoeffer was born in 1906 to a well-educated, well-off family and became a Lutheran minister in Germany. In 1930 he visited America and was appalled with how American industrialists were treating coal miners and black farmers, which he wrote about extensively in his letters and journals. Later when Hitler rose to power, many of the Christian churches backed and blessed the Nazi regime, but this disgusted Bonhoeffer, who began a movement within the church to reject Nazism and continued to speak out about morals and ethics.

But after six years of preaching against Nazism, Bonhoeffer began to feel that words alone were not enough to produce change. He would have to act. He became involved with a group of German military intelligence who were smuggling Jews out of Germany and scheming to kill Hitler with a bomb in the now infamous July 20 plot. In 1943, Bonhoeffer was arrested for his role in smuggling, then when Hitler learned in 1944 that Bonhoeffer had been involved in the July 20 plot, he had him hung in a concentration camp.

While Bonhoeffer was imprisoned, he wrote some of his most profound sermons. "The ultimate question for a responsible man to ask is not how he is to extricate himself heroically from the affair, but how the coming generation is to live," he reminded us all, but especially the Rebels. The Rebel has a knack for breaking out of sticky situations, but he grows when he accepts restrictions, detention, exile, and even death for the sake of the greater good and overcomes injustice with truth-telling.

Nelson Mandela shares a similar story to Bonhoeffer. He, too, in his young adulthood resorted to sabotage and property violence as a response to apartheid in South Africa. Then he spent 27 years in prison, emerging wiser and stronger than before. "As I walked out the door toward the gate that would lead to my freedom," Mandela said, "I knew if I didn't leave my bitterness and hatred behind, I'd still be in prison." He was elected South Africa's first black president in 1990, and he could have sought revenge or self-interest, but instead he launched a movement for truth and reconciliation in South Africa to inspire people to forgive and be able to cooperate with each other to rebuild and revitalize the nation.

Did you know if it weren't for Rebel protestants, the Bible might still only be widely available in Latin? In the Middle Ages one of the biggest crime of the early protestant movement, at least in the eyes of the very powerful Roman Catholic Church, was translating the Bible into the "common" languages. In 1229 the Pope made it illegal for "laypeople" to even possess a Bible. Then in the 1380s a Rebel named John Wycliffe was the first to ever completely translate the Bible into English, and not only did the Catholic Church publicly burn the Wycliffe Bible, they dug up Wycliffe's bones after he died and burned them too! And this burning of books and heretics at the stake went on for hundreds of years.

In fact, the Vatican is the number one burner of Bibles in history, mostly because they wanted the population to rely on the priests and the Pope for all spiritual guidance. Because of the widespread persecution of non-Catholic Christians in Central Europe, my own Huguenot ancestors, the Chasteigners, left France in 1699 to come to America where we went all different directions preaching the gospel.

My 7th great grandfather John "Ten Shilling Bell" Chastain founded the first Baptist Church in Tennessee, and what parishioners remembered most about him was that he had a beautiful singing voice — like a ten-shilling bell — and he washed their feet, something that was outrageously rebellious in the Victorian age, when bare ankles were scandalous, but especially because the Chasteigners were old French aristocracy, cousins of the Capetian Dynasty.

Guess who else is known for his beautiful singing voice and remembered for washing his parishioners' feet, which even in the 90s was a rebellion against the norm? My dad. Funny story... Before we knew the history of our ancestors, we took a church group to the very first church in Tennessee. When reading the signs with the history written on them, a deacon said, "Hey Brother Eddie, I wonder if you and this John Chastain guy are related."

Dad replied, "Well, if we are, then according to my granddad, he spelled his name wrong! There have always been two Es in Chasteen."

As it turns out, we all spell our name wrong! But my grandfather was right that there always were two Es in Chasteigner, and he was rebellious enough to not let anyone tell him otherwise!

By the 20th century the Rebel archetypes within the protestant Christian church became the largest distributors of Bibles in world history. One particular American group was founded in 1899 in Wisconsin and became known as the Gideons. Through the cooperation and coalition of a quarter of a million men in 190 countries, they have distributed to date more than 2.5 billion Bibles worldwide in over 100 languages using only volunteer efforts.

Groups like the Gideons and others didn't just distribute Bibles to spite the Pope, though. They were driven by a cause — to liberate the hearts and minds of people who may be at their lowest moment through the tender power of scriptures. This is why so many Gideon Bibles were placed in spaces like hospitals, jail cells, and hotel rooms — where people are likely to be hurting, burdened, or alone. Their rebellion succeeded not because they fought fire with fire to try to burn down the system, but because they coalesced around a cause to build a new and better system they envisioned for the future, one Bible at a time.

Ironically, the Gideons group was named after a Rebel of the Old Testament book of Judges named Gideon whom God calls to fight off oppressive raiders from a neighboring empire, despite the fact that Gideon was the youngest member of the weakest clan. The raiders themselves were ruthless and had been getting away with pillaging the crops and people of the tribes of Israel. When God shows up to call Gideon "mighty man of valor," Gideon basically replies, "Who? Me?" Gideon not only questions God — imagine that, a Rebel questioning authority — but he also asks God to give him multiple signs so that he will work up the courage to lead the rebellion against the raiders. But even though Gideon questioned God, he also proved he was willing to cooperate with God, even when the plan led Gideon toward doing what he did not want to do because he believed in the cause of liberating his people.

For example, the first thing God tells Gideon to do is tear down his father's altar to Baal, the foreign god of the raiders. Gideon was afraid, so he tore down the altar at night, but he still complied. When Gideon organizes a party of 32,000 men to fight beside him against the raiders, God says, "Nah, that's too many. Send any home that are afraid." Much to Gideon's dismay, 22,000 men went home. Then God said, "Still too many." God instructed Gideon to test the men, and only 300 passed the test. God told Gideon to send the rest home. He complied again.

Finally God told Gideon to take the 300 men in the night to the raiders' camp and instead of bringing swords to slay them, bring trumpets to blow, torches to wave, and jars and pots to smash. Imagine being Gideon in this moment, facing an entire camp of ruthless raiders with only 300 men and some clay pots and trumpets. Nevertheless Gideon cooperated with God's plan, and the raiders were so surprised and afraid that they brought their own self-destruction in the chaos.

There is a lesson here for the Rebel. I'll let you decide what it is.

Reflection

We're reaching the end of our journey together, so at this point, I'm sure you know the drill — let's reflect on ways to heal and strengthen our inner Rebel:

- Think about how you respond to: unjust authority, unnecessary demands, and unwarranted restrictions. Are your responses external like the Anarchist or internal like the Dissident?
- Is your defiance generally based on a cause outside of yourself? If so, what is the cause that drives you? If not, consider what bitterness is driving your defiance-for-defiance's sake. Hint: It probably has to do with your inner child not being free.
- How can you be more cooperative toward friends or family who could potentially work with you to bring about a liberating change or small scale revolution? Have you shared with them the cause that drives you? Why or why not?

Chapter Summary

- Theme: Change and Revolution
- Key to Growth: Cooperation and Cause
- Essence: The Rebel is not afraid to challenge norms, shake up the status quo, and "fight the power" for what they believe is right. They drive change and inspire others to see beyond restrictions and limitations to bring liberation.
- Pitfall to Avoid: Defiance without reason or cause; isolationism
- Growth Focus: Embracing cooperation, using rebellion constructively (to advance a cause), and pursuing change with empathy and heart.

12

The Creator

Overview

- **Description:** The Creator embodies imagination, innovation, and self-expression. He is the archetype of artistry and the drive to bring new things into the world.
- **Major Conflict:** The Creator struggles with perfectionism and pride. He risks becoming either paralyzed by self-doubt (Perfectionist) or overly self-important (Vain).
- **Path to Growth:** The Creator grows by embracing imperfection, sharing his gifts with the world, and using his creativity to inspire and uplift others.

Stories of the Creator

"Every creator painfully experiences the chasm between his inner vision and its ultimate expression." – Isaac Bashevis Singer

"Come with me... and you'll be... in a world of pure imagination... take a look, and you'll see into your imagination. We'll begin with a spin, traveling in the world of my creation. What we see will defy explanation." This stanza from the famous Willy Wonka & the Chocolate Factory song was the first thing that popped into my head when I sat down to write this chapter. Did you know this song, sung by the legend Gene Wilder, was written and recorded in a day, and when it was released, it was originally a flop?

But after Gene passed, the number of streams of "Pure Imagination" shot up over a thousand percent, in tribute to his memory and legacy. Gene Wilder was certainly a Creator (and a Joker). Not only did he act and sing, he wrote, directed, and was deeply involved in the creative process. One of his quotes particularly speaks to the Creator archetype: "The thing I love about making movies is the peace of mind that I know I don't have to be perfect the first time. I can be perfect the second time or the third time." While this quote is amusing, when considered alongside the story of "Pure Imagination", it also conveys a truth: practice makes perfect, but timing makes popular. More on that later.

First let's talk about what defines the Creator. The Creator archetype makes something from his imagination turn into reality. Many times this archetype shows up as an artist or a musician, but not always. Writers, architects, chefs, engineers and more use their imaginations to create. Even Arnold Schwarzenegger is a man that I would classify as a Creator type because he created his dream physique and turned his imaginations of being Mr. Universe, a leading man in film, and Governor of California all into reality! The gift of this archetype is being able to express the dreams and visions from inside your own heart and mind so that others may see (or hear, taste, smell, touch) your creations and become inspired.

From Willy Wonka to Tony Stark, Creator types are iconized in media as eccentric loners, often self-absorbed yet passionately devoted to their craft, usually above all else. But only toxic Creators isolate themselves. Willy Wonka shows us the first way Creators become toxic: perfectionism. Tony Stark shows us the second way Creators become toxic: self-importance. Let's talk about it.

One of my favorite quotes about perfectionism is from Don Miguel Ruiz. He said, "To be authentic is to be at peace with your own imperfections." Toxic people believe that the only way to be good is to be perfect. Even in the process of writing this book, I had to stand up to multiple people (usually women) who wanted to argue that John F. Kennedy was **not**, in fact, a "good" man because he allegedly had extra-marital affairs. They clearly haven't read Jackie's memoirs. But it really is as Voltaire said, "Perfect is the enemy of good." The longing and striving for perfection only masks a deep insecurity and self-doubt that your best effort isn't good enough. However, to paraphrase Don Miguel Ruiz in his book The Voice of Knowledge: what if the biggest lie we've ever been told is "nobody's perfect" when the truth is — we all are?

The way the Perfectionist Creator is redeemed is by realizing perfection is entirely subjective. The character of the Beast from Beauty and the Beast teaches us about the Perfectionist shadow. The Beast believes that because he is imperfect (a.k.a. physically ugly) that there is nothing good about himself or the life he has created. He believes he will never be loved. Belle teaches him that he doesn't have to be perfect to be loved and that he, in fact, is perfect to her in the present moment because of his great kindness and generosity. His acceptance of her love is what redeems him — when he realizes that beauty is in the eye of the beholder. The Perfectionist Creator must learn that while they cannot be everything to everyone, to someone they are everything, just as they are.

For an historic and tragic example of the Perfectionist, look no further than Vincent Van Gogh. In spite of his artistic brilliance and devotion to his craft (he was said to have made at least one painting per day!), he constantly questioned his worth as an artist and a man, often resorting to destroying countless numbers of his own paintings from being haunted by inadequacy. They just weren't good enough for him. During his life, he sold only one painting and had no formal recognition. He is quoted as saying, "I put my heart and my soul into my work, and have lost my mind in the process." Eventually he had a break down and was institutionalized. At age 37, Vincent Van Gogh passed away from a gunshot wound, likely self-inflicted, never knowing that people in the future would flock to museums to see his work on display and feel inspired by its beauty. His work wasn't perfect to him, but it is perfect to us.

The second way a Creator becomes toxic is by becoming self-absorbed and self-important, otherwise known as: vain. The Vain Creator mostly creates for themselves, by themselves — refusing both direction and criticism. They claim to be "self-taught" but won't tell you they're practically unteachable. Their sizable ego is usually built as a coping mechanism in early childhood that compels them to exude outer confidence as cover of their inner sense of incompetence. However it can also be that the Vain Creator has been spoiled, that is, excessively praised. The antidote for this poison is the same: service.

The Vain Creator must learn that the act of creation is to benefit others, not just gratify themselves by collecting praise and validation. Tony Stark from Iron Man is the perfect fictional example of the Vain Creator. When we meet Tony, he is an egomaniac, obsessed with his work and himself. He's a wealthy playboy who takes his closest friends for granted. Is he a creative genius? No doubt about it. Is he toxic? Also yes. It's often said of the Vain Creator that they have a "god complex". He uses invention to try to make himself invulnerable, immortal even, while selling weapons systems that bring violence and death around the world.

In his vanity, Tony frequently "plays god" - such as when he used the Mind Stone to create his world-peacekeeping AI: Ultron. While Tony intended for Ultron to be a "suit of armor around the world," what he actually created was a twisted mirror of his own Shadow. Through his certainty of directive and opposition to weakness (both programmed into him by Stark), Ultron becomes genocidal and believes the only way to save planet Earth is to facilitate the extinction of the human race. The Ultron disaster shakes Tony to his core and causes a rift between himself and the other Avengers. Interestingly, this is also when Tony creates Vision - an AI robot that was everything Ultron was not, and everything Tony needed to become to rise from toxicity.

The Creator archetype holds particular tension around the ideas of good and bad. Where the Perfectionist Creator thinks too little of themselves and their work (bad), the Vain Creator thinks too much of themselves and their work (good). The Perfectionist Creator views their work as not good enough. The Vain Creator views their work as not bad in any way. Think about that. The key lesson here for the Creators is that good and bad coexist and are highly subjective. There is good in every bad, just like there is bad in every good. The "Pure Imagination" song from the first of this chapter is an example of this — in the beginning, it was judged as a flop (bad), but later it became an anthem of nostalgia and memoriam (good).

One way that the Creator learns to see the world through a more neutral moral lens is through service to others. Serving others is not complicated. Any time you perform an action that helps another person, that is an act of service. Sandra Bullock said in an interview on CBS Mornings that she thinks everyone should be a waiter or waitress — a server of food and drinks — at least once in their life. This is especially true for the Creator archetypes. When Creators serve others, it breaks the illusion that perfection is the highest valued outcome. The reality is that **helpfulness** is usually the highest valued outcome.

Service doesn't have to be perfect to be helpful. Having worked many years in food service myself, I can tell you it taught me how to be more conscientious of ways I could help others and how to make mistakes with grace and gentleness toward myself. When you have a section of eight 6-top tables that are all full, and it's happy hour on a holiday weekend, mistakes and delays will happen — but there is ZERO time to dwell on it. You have to learn to take mistakes and failures in stride, focus on helping the client with their needs (e.g. hunger), and face the reality that literally no one is perfect. All we ever can do is our best in the moment.

Food service work also teaches you that you can be the best, most perfect server, and some people still just won't tip you over $5. This customer, too, is breaking the illusion that perfection is the highest valued outcome. They're also teaching the Creators that bad and good are all subjective. Maybe that customer really thought $5 was a good tip. By contrast, one night while working at a steakhouse serving a 6-top table of three couples celebrating their anniversaries together, everything went wrong that could go wrong. Their reservation wasn't ready on time, the kitchen was behind, some of the food was wrong when it came out — I would have rated my level of service as BAD. In fact, I felt so bad about it all that I got permission from my manager to give each couple a little bouquet of flowers from the tables as an apology. And would you believe that was the biggest tip I ever received? This taught me such a valuable lesson: that my value is not tied to my perfection and that perfection is in the eye of the beholder, just like beauty.

If you're on social media, you'll see more Creator types with the Vain Shadow than with the Perfectionist Shadow, which is why "influencer culture" is imbued with self-absorption. The reason the Perfectionists don't show up as often is because they're too paralyzed by self-doubt to even post their content. The way to grow out of this toxicity is... you guessed it! SERVICE. When people create content from a place of service (i.e. how can I help?), the internet simply cannot get enough.

There is a guy on TikTok who goes around doing volunteer landscaping on abandoned or overgrown properties where the property owner is somehow unable to care for the lawn. His business name is "SB Mowing" (@sbmowing) if you want to look him up. His work is not perfect, but it is so **good** that it has earned him 14.5 million followers to date. This is a modern day example of a nontoxic Creator. He imagines better looking yards and makes them reality on behalf of the neighbors to help improve everyone's property values. Turning imagination into reality to help others is the Creator's gift.

It was for this reason that I saved the story of John 2:1-11 for the Creator Jesus section. If you don't know this scripture reference it's the story of Jesus turning water into wine for his mother at a wedding in Cana. If Jesus had a Perfectionist Shadow, he might have been riddled with doubt about doing this. I mean, the law did speak ill of drunkenness — what about his reputation? Or what if he was worried the wedding-goers wouldn't like his wine? If Jesus had a Vain Shadow, he might have boasted about the quality of his wine instead. But when you revisit this story you find Jesus being modest and even secretive about his creation. The "master of the banquet" commented on how good the wine was, and Jesus stayed quiet about his act of service. This showcases how when the Creator becomes truly nontoxic, they create for care not for credit.

This brings us to another way that Creators grow: by understanding that timing is important, but not more important than serving. When Mary approaches Jesus to tell him they need more wine, he replies to her, "Woman, why do you involve me? My hour has not yet come." (NIV, John 2:4). It makes me laugh that Mary doesn't even respond to him and just directs the servants to do whatever Jesus says. Jesus understood that creation shouldn't be rushed and that timing is important for a good reception, but that it's also ok to act before you are fully ready if you're being called to serve.

As a creator, sometimes you might hesitate to put yourself out there — you might grapple with, "Is it the right time?" But the truth is that procrastination is the tool of the Perfectionist. Seneca the Stoic philosopher said: "Luck is what happens when preparation meets opportunity." We can never know when the time will be exactly right, but we can be creating good work until the timing aligns. If you're hesitant to share your creative endeavors, start by seeking out a way to serve with your craft and share that process instead. It will give you confidence and motivation to continue to share your imagination and creation.

A.A. Gill once said, "So much of life is not about whether you're good or bad, or right or wrong, or can afford or not afford - it's just about timing." All Creators should realize this in order to overcome their need for popularity as validation of their "goodness." Unlike Jesus, we don't have a direct line to knowing divine timing, so all we can really do is create in service and pray that our creation will help someone exactly at the right time for them. One of my favorite things about creating helpful content on TikTok is when someone comments on an old post saying, "I needed this today." We truly never know when the timing will be just right for our creations to become popular or "go viral." All we can ever do is observe trends and take guesses about timing and interest.

Sometimes I make a video that I think is perfect timing, and only 300 people see it. Other times I make a video on a whim, and 300,000 people see it. I like to remind myself that if 300 people were in a room with me, I wouldn't think it was such a small number then. But what I've learned through the process of creation is that the only real formula for success is authenticity plus consistency, showing up and creating the videos whether the timing is perfect or not. It's like Wayne Gretzky told us, "You miss 100% of the shots you don't take."

When the Creator is worried about timing or popularity, it takes away from their authenticity. Authenticity is when you show up fully as yourself and create what is aligned with your unique imagination. Vincent Van Gogh, in spite of his Shadow, was deeply authentic. He could have never imagined his works would bring inspiration and joy to millions of people, spanning generations, but he kept on creating in spite of his relative obscurity and unpopularity during his lifetime.

The Creator creates even when no one is looking because one day their creation might show up just at the right time to bless someone. They seek to serve humanity through imagination even when no one seems to notice or appreciate them. There's a quote by Morgan Harper Nichols that says, "Tell the story of the mountain you climbed. Your words could become a page in someone else's survival guide." The Creator must realize that what they have learned and/or can express might help the next person who is on a similar path but two or three steps behind, and helping just one person makes the creation worth sharing.

If you're still struggling to understand how to be of service to others using your unique imagination, then I challenge you to think about something you've created that has garnered the most gratitude from others. Gratitude is a more important metric than praise or recognition. When people express sincere thankfulness for something you created, make a note! Over time, you'll see a pattern that could help you create a personal brand for your creative endeavors, confident that your craft is helpful to others in some way or another.

The word "help" means to "make it easier for someone to do something." How we provide value as Creators is by making something easier for others through our imagination. In the case of visual art or music, this seems a little confusing, but consider how music makes it easier to dance or even concentrate or become absorbed in cinema. Visual art often makes it easier to remember a moment in time or that beauty exists even in the darkest days. The surest sign that you have helped someone or "made something easier" for them is that they will thank you. Gratitude is an indicator of your talents for service.

At first, the immature Creator creates to help themselves — to express their emotion, to release or prove something, to find identity or meaning. Later, the mature Creator reframes creation as a way to meet others needs or solve common problems (service). The Perfectionist wonders, "Will the audience love me?" The Vain Creator exclaims, "I need to say this!" But the nontoxic Creator says, "How can I love the audience through my work?" and, "Who might need to hear this?" This focus on service and authenticity is what helps the Creator grow in both influence and value.

Reflection

I can't believe we've reached the end. Thank you so much for reading all these stories along with me. What a wild ride, with probably one too many Star Wars references, I'll admit. Before you go, though, let's reflect on cultivating the energy of the Creator:

- Do you lean toward perfectionism or vainglorious pride? How can you lean into service with your craft to help you break free from the illusion of good versus bad?

- What has produced "raving fans" in your life — that is people who are sincerely appreciative and enthusiastic about your creations? How can you leverage that talent or gift to help more people?
- In your day to day life, when do you find yourself imagining how something could be better? Have you acted to turn your imagination into reality? If not, why are you hesitant?

Chapter Summary

- Theme: Innovation and Expression
- Key to Growth: Service and Authenticity
- Essence: The Creator archetype is imaginative and driven to bring something new into reality. They find fulfillment in self-expression that helps others.
- Pitfall to Avoid: Perfectionism or vanity
- Growth Focus: Embracing imperfection, sharing unique gifts without self-doubt, and focusing on how to help others rather than how to become popular

Epilogue

This is not farewell forever, just goodbye for now.

There are so many good men who didn't get included in these pages simply because I didn't want to write an entire set of MENcyclopedias... lol... So just know this is not a comprehensive list, only a starting point to inspire us to think deeply about what it means to be masculine. I hope you recognized men you know and love in these stories, and I'd love to hear from you if you did.

If you're interested in more of my stories, check out my blog — gardenvarietyblog.com — or find me on social media at Garden Variety Jess.

I'm also planning on releasing an app with an archetype quiz that will not only tell you the top three archetypes that you most match, but also suggest quests for your personal growth. Stay tuned at nontoxicmen.org for more on that!

For further reading, consider the following works:

- King, Warrior, Magician, Lover by Robert Moore and Douglas Gillette
- Of Boys and Men by Richard Reeves
- Awakening the Heroes Within by Carol S. Pearson
- Man and His Symbols by Carl Jung
- Archetypes: Who Are You? by Caroline Myss
- The Will to Change by bell hooks
- All About Love by bell hooks
- The Four Agreements by Don Miguel Ruiz
- The Voice of Knowledge by Don Miguel Ruiz

About the Author

Jessica Chasteen comes from a long line of independent Baptist ministers dating back to 1699, but her calling led her to heal through stories rather than sermons. A writer, teacher, and avid gardener, she discovered that the same principles that help plants thrive can help people break destructive cycles and grow into their fullest potential.

Known as Garden Variety Jess to her devoted social media following, Jessica combines psychological insight with practical wisdom, creating content that educates, entertains, and empowers. When she's not writing, telling tall tales about conspiracy theories, or tending her farm with her dogs, she's helping men recognize their strength and step into healthy masculinity.